W9-CFB-953

SERVING LGBT YOUTH
IN OUT-OF-HOME CARE

CWLA
Best
Practice
Guidelines

SHANNAN WILBER,
CAITLIN RYAN, AND
JODY MARKSAMER

CHILD WELFARE LEAGUE OF AMERICA
ARLINGTON, VA

The Child Welfare League of America is the nation's oldest and largest membership-based child welfare organization. We are committed to engaging people everywhere in promoting the well-being of children, youth, and their families, and protecting every child from harm.

© 2006 by the Child Welfare League of America, Inc. All rights reserved. Neither this book nor any part may be reproduced or transmitted in any form or by any means, electronic or mechanical, including photocopying, microfilming, and recording, or by any information storage and retrieval system, without permission in writing from the publisher. For information on this or other CWLA publications, contact the CWLA Publications Department at the address below.

CHILD WELFARE LEAGUE OF AMERICA, INC.
www.cwla.org

CURRENT PRINTING (last digit)
10 9 8 7 6 5 4 3

Cover and text design by Jennifer R. Geanakos
Edited by Julie Gwin

Printed in the United States of America

ISBN- 978-1-58760-095-1

Library of Congress Cataloging-in-Publication Data

Best practice guidelines : serving LGBT youth in out-of-home care/ Shannan Wilber, Caitlin Ryan, and Jody Marksamer.
    p. cm.
  Includes bibliographical references.
  ISBN 1-58760-095-1 (alk. paper)
    1. Gay youth—Services for—United States. 2. Lesbian youth—Services for—United States. 3. Bisexual youth—Services for—United States. 4. Transsexuals—Services for—United States. I. Ryan, Caitlin. II. Marksamer, Jody. III. Title. IV. Title: LGBT youth. V. Title: Lesbian, gay, bisexual and transgender youth.

HV1449.W545 2006
362.73'3086640973—dc22   2006012399

Contents

Acknowledgments

The Model Standards Project was made possible through the generous support of the Annie E. Casey Foundation, the B'Charta B'Chaim Fund of the Tides Foundation, the Evelyn & Walter Haas Jr. Fund, the Kevin J. Mossier Foundation, the Stuart Foundation, and an anonymous donor.

Introduction

During the past decade, lesbian, gay, bisexual, and transgender (LGBT) adolescents have become increasingly visible in our families, communities, and systems of care. A significant number of these youth are in the custody of child welfare or juvenile justice agencies. Yet the public systems that are charged with their care and well-being have been unresponsive to their needs and slow to acknowledge that LGBT children and adolescents are in urgent need of appropriate and equitable care (see, for example, Mallon, 1992, 1994, 1998). Child welfare and juvenile justice systems have not incorporated advances in research and understanding related to human sexuality and child and adolescent development that have informed the development of professional standards and guidelines for the major professional associations. As a result, these systems continue to deliver misguided, uninformed, second-class care to LGBT youth in their custody.

With few exceptions, policies and professional standards governing services to youth in out-of-home care fail to consider the young people's sexual orientation or gender identity. The lack of leadership and professional guidance related to these key developmental issues has left a vacuum that is often filled by harmful and discriminatory practices based on personal biases related to adolescent sexuality and gender identity rather than informed, evidence-based policies and guidelines. The institutional legacy of systemic failure to provide informed guidance on these issues is reflected in disturbingly common practices:

- A child welfare worker considers a young gay boy unadoptable solely because of his sexual orientation.

- Line staff in a group home fail to intervene when residents harass and abuse a transgender youth because they believe he "asked for it" by being open about his gender identity.

- Relative caregivers send a lesbian teen to a counselor for reparative therapy in a misguided attempt to try change her sexual orientation, even though the major professional associations, including the American Psychiatric Association and the American Academy of Pediatrics, specifically caution against this practice.

- Detention facility staff place a gay youth in isolation "for his own protection," depriving him of education, recreation, companionship, or other programming and services.

- Foster parents ridicule and demean a young boy in their custody whom they perceive to be effeminate, calling him a sissy and exhorting him to "stop acting like a girl."

- Child welfare personnel repeatedly move a lesbian youth from one inappropriate placement to another, subjecting her to constant rejection and discrimination and depriving her of a permanent home or family.

- A transgender girl refuses to shower with the boys in her detention unit because she is afraid for her safety. The facility will not allow her to have private shower time, even though she has reported ongoing abuse and threats of violence from the boys, and so she does not shower.

The Model Standards: A Historical Framework

In 2002, Legal Services for Children[1] and the National Center for Lesbian Rights[2] launched the Model Standards Project, a multiyear project to develop and disseminate model professional standards governing services to LGBT youth in out-of-home care. The project grew out of staff members' direct experience working with LGBT youth and their families, as well as inquiries from LGBT youth across the country who shared distressing and discriminatory experiences they had in out-of-home care, and from service providers who sought guidance on how best to respond to these situations and guidelines for providing appropriate care for these vulnerable children and adolescents.

The goal of the Model Standards Project is to improve services and outcomes by giving child welfare and juvenile justice agencies accurate,

---

[1] Legal Services for Children, Inc. (LSC), founded in 1975, provides direct legal representation and social work services to children and youth in the San Francisco Bay Area. LSC's mission is to provide free legal and social services to children and youth to stabilize their lives and help them realize their full potential. LSC's Queer Youth Legal Services project provides legal and social work services to lesbian, gay, bisexual, and transgender youth. For more information about LSC, see www.lsc-sf.org.

[2] The National Center for Lesbian Rights (NCLR) is a national legal resource center committed to advancing the rights and safety of LGBT people and their families through litigation, public policy advocacy, and public education. NCLR, founded in 1977, serves more than 5,000 LGBT people—including youth—in all 50 states and several countries each year. NCLR's Safe Homes Project is specifically focused on advocating for LGBT youth in state care. For more information about NCLR, see www.nclrights.org.

up-to-date information about the best practices for providing competent services to LGBT youth, based on the knowledge and practical experience of experts
in the field. Project staff (see Appendix A) conducted a series of focus groups
and interviews with LGBT youth involved in child welfare and juvenile justice
systems across the country. Staff also convened a national advisory committee
(see Appendix B) composed of individuals with direct experience in public agencies serving youth, including young people with direct systems experience and
child welfare and juvenile justice professionals with specific interest and expert-
ise in the concerns of LGBT youth. In consultation with Advisory Committee
members, project staff developed a draft set of standards, which they pilot-
tested in workshops and trainings nationally. The best practice guidelines
published in this volume grew out of the Model Standards Project.

A few concerned child welfare professionals created the foundation for
the Model Standards Project more than 25 years ago when they identified
major unmet needs of lesbian, gay, and gender-nonconforming youth and
worked to develop responsive programs to address these systemic gaps in
care. These efforts led to the development of Gay and Lesbian Adolescent
Social Services (GLASS)—the nation's first group home for LGBT youth—
which Teresa DeCrescenzo founded in Los Angeles in 1984. Three years
later, Gary Mallon developed specialized child welfare services, including a
residential program, for lesbian and gay youth at Green Chimneys
Children's Services in New York City. Over the years, GLASS and Green
Chimneys have expanded their programs and now provide a range of
services to LGBT youth in state custody, including foster care, mentoring,
education, health care, transitional services, and residential care.

Building on the pioneering work of Mallon, DeCrescenzo, and their col-
leagues, a growing number of committed child welfare professionals have developed programs and models of intervention that are inclusive of and responsive to
the needs of LGBT youth. Initially, these programs operated in relative isolation
and focused primarily on specialized residential services in which lesbian and gay
youth could live and learn in safe, supportive environments. In recent years, these
efforts have moved toward a more integrated model that supports a wide range
of inclusive, safe, and nondiscriminatory services to LGBT youth. National
initiatives have helped coordinate these efforts and support the development of
a professional consensus regarding the critical elements of systems reform.

In 2002, the Child Welfare League of America (CWLA)—the nation's oldest
child welfare professional organization—joined the Lambda Legal Education and

Defense Fund to create the Fostering Transitions Project. Over the course of three years, the project sponsored a series of regional forums in 13 jurisdictions across the country. In each location, project staff convened youth, caregivers, child welfare workers, legal professionals, and other interested individuals to discuss the experiences of LGBT youth in foster care and to make recommendations for systemic reforms. A network of almost 100 child welfare professionals and LGBT youth guide the CWLA/Lambda project. The Advisory Network shares resources, discusses programmatic challenges and opportunities, and collaborates on local, state, and national child welfare policy issues. The Fostering Transitions Project has published a report summarizing the findings of the regional "listening forums" and making recommendations aimed at child welfare policymakers and practitioners (CWLA & Lambda Legal, 2006).

In 2002, Caitlin Ryan developed the Family Acceptance Project[3] with Rafael Diaz at San Francisco State University to study the effects of family and caregiver acceptance and rejection on the health, mental health, and well-being of LGBT youth. Designed as a community research, intervention, and training initiative, the project has generated extensive findings on LGBT youth living in a range of family and out-of-home settings, including homeless adolescents and foster youth and their families. The authors have used the findings from the Family Acceptance Project to inform and frame the scope of the Model Standards Project and best practice guidelines.

These national efforts, as well as the best practice guidelines contained in this volume, are supported by an emerging legal framework defining the constitutional and statutory obligations of public systems serving LGBT youth in out-of-home care. In 2003, a young transgender woman won a landmark lawsuit against the New York City Administration for Children's Services requiring the child welfare agency to permit her to wear female attire in her all-boys group home (*Doe v. Bell*, 2003).[4] The same year, California passed a state law—the first of its kind in the country—that

---

[3]   The Family Acceptance Project is a multiyear research, intervention, and training initiative on LGBT youth and their families and caregivers carried out at the César E. Chávez Institute at San Francisco State University. For more information about the project, see http://familyproject.sfsu.edu.

[4]   Plaintiff argued that prohibiting her from wearing dresses and skirts caused her great psychological distress and amounted to illegal discrimination on the basis of her disability (gender identity disorder) and gender under the New York State housing nondiscrimination law, as well as a violation of her First Amendment freedom of expression. The court agreed and ordered the Administration for Children's Services to make reasonable accommodations to allow her to dress and otherwise present herself consistently with her female gender identity.

explicitly prohibits discrimination in the foster care system on the basis of sexual orientation and gender identity.[5] In 2005, the Kansas Supreme Court struck down a state statute that imposed harsher punishment for voluntary sexual conduct between youth of the same sex than the punishment imposed for the same conduct between youth of the opposite sex (*State v. Limon*, 2005).[6] In a 2006 civil rights case challenging the treatment of LGBT youth confined in Hawaii's youth correctional facility, the federal district court found that isolating LGBT youth for their protection and failing to protect them from ongoing abuse and harassment violates due process (*RG v. Koller*, 2006).[7]

The Scope of the Guidelines

The best practice guidelines contained in this volume provide direction to agencies responsible for the care of LGBT youth in out-of-home care. For several reasons, the authors have intentionally chosen to address these guidelines to both child welfare and juvenile justice professionals. First, significant overlap exists between the populations of young people served by these two systems (Weithorn, 2005). Children and youth who are subjected to family abuse or neglect often engage in behaviors that may also bring them to the attention of the juvenile justice system. This is equally true for LGBT youth, who experience social marginalization that places them at heightened risk of involvement in the child welfare and juvenile justice

---

[5] Under the California Foster Care Non-discrimination Act, all foster youth and people who provide care and services to foster youth in California have the right to fair and equal access to all available child welfare services, placements, care, treatment, and benefits, and to be free from discrimination or harassment on the basis of actual or perceived race, ethnic group identification, ancestry, national origin, color, religion, sex, sexual orientation, gender identity, mental or physical disability, or HIV status. Because training is crucial to enable service providers to fulfill their responsibilities to provide safe and nondiscriminatory care, placement, and services to foster youth, this law also mandates initial and ongoing training for all group home administrators, foster parents, and department licensing personnel (Cal. Welf. & Inst. Code § 16001.9[a][22]).

[6] The state statute at issue in *Limon*, known as the "Romeo and Juliet" law, made the penalty for statutory rape less severe when the case involved two teenagers, but only if they were members of the opposite sex. The case involved a consensual sexual encounter between two boys who were residents of a home for developmentally delayed youth. Because the Romeo and Juliet law excluded sexual acts between members of the same sex, the older youth was charged under the adult criminal sodomy statute. The court imposed a sentence of more than 17 years, although a teen charged with engaging in the same conduct but with a teen of the opposite sex would have received a maximum of 15 months. After a lengthy and complex appeals process, during which the young defendant served more than five years in prison, the Kansas Supreme Court found that the statute violated the Equal Protection Clause of the federal constitution.

[7] *RG v. Koller* was filed on behalf of three youth who had been confined at the Hawaii Youth Correctional Facility and alleged that they had been subjected to ongoing harassment and abuse by wards and staff because of their known or perceived sexual orientation and gender identity. The court granted a preliminary injunction requiring the defendants to refrain from harassing, abusing, discriminating against, or isolating the plaintiffs based on their actual or perceived sexual orientation or gender identity, and from failing to protect the youth from anti-LGBT peer harassment and abuse.

systems. Indeed, many of the youth who participated in focus groups to help develop these guidelines reported having been involved in both systems.

Secondly, the guidelines are grounded in a youth development approach that provides services and supports designed to promote young people's competencies and connect them to families and communities (Mallon, 1997). LGBT youth in out-of-home care need these same supports and services regardless of the system in which they are involved. Although the purposes of child welfare and juvenile justice systems differ in some respects, both seek to promote young people's healthy development into well-adjusted, productive adults. The guidelines address this common purpose by identifying the core elements of appropriate services to all LGBT youth in out-of-home care.

Finally, the guidelines attempt to address the dearth of scholarship and professional attention to the needs of LGBT youth involved in the juvenile justice system. To date, virtually all of the scholarship and policy development related to LGBT youth in care has been directed at reform of the child welfare system. These efforts have resulted in significant progress toward the acknowledgment and understanding of LGBT children and youth in foster care. Researchers have paid very little attention, however, to the ways in which juvenile justice agencies must adjust to meet the needs of LGBT youth in their custody. The wholesale failure of the juvenile justice profession to address these issues has resulted in conditions and practices that subject LGBT youth to pervasive discrimination and serious emotional and physical harm. These guidelines provide a tool to begin the process of addressing these systemic deficiencies.

The guidelines also address both sexual orientation and gender identity. Although LGBT youth need the same essential opportunities and supports, transgender and gender-nonconforming youth confront unique challenges that child welfare and juvenile justice professionals need to understand. Nonetheless, with few exceptions (DeCrescenzo & Mallon, 2000; Mallon, 1999d; Ryan & Diaz, 2005), the existing literature and research focus on lesbian, gay, and bisexual youth and do not address the needs of transgender youth. Again, the absence of professional dialogue and attention to issues specific to transgender youth has contributed to policies and practices that subject transgender youth to pervasive discrimination and abuse.[8]

---

[8]   Unless otherwise noted, the discussion, as well as the recommendations, contained in the guidelines applies equally to lesbian, gay, bisexual, and transgender youth. The text specifies when research, programs, and recommendations pertain only to sexual orientation or gender identity.

Juvenile justice and child welfare professionals can use these guidelines:

- to support the development of policies and practices governing the care of LGBT youth in out-of-home care;

- to create training materials for agency personnel, facility staff, care-givers, and providers; and

- to provide guidance to professionals and caregivers serving individual LGBT youth in out-of-home care.

The guidelines are divided into eight topical chapters. Chapter 1 describes the process by which LGBT youth become aware of their sexual orientation or gender identity; the experiences and social conditions that may contribute to, or deepen, their involvement in the child welfare and juvenile justice systems; and the mistreatment and discrimination to which they are frequently subjected in out-of-home care.

Chapter 2 recommends specific practices and policies to help child welfare and juvenile justice agencies create and maintain an inclusive organizational culture in which the inherent worth and dignity of every person is respected and in which every person is treated fairly and equally.

Chapter 3 emphasizes the importance of family connections for LGBT youth. The chapter discusses the challenges confronting contemporary LGBT youth and their families, and it describes the steps child welfare and juvenile justice agencies can take to preserve families, whenever possible, and to create and support permanent connections for LGBT youth who cannot reconcile with their birthfamilies.

Chapter 4 describes the obligation of agencies to promote the health and well-being of LGBT youth in their care by supporting the development and integration of their sexual orientation and gender identity, prohibiting practices that pathologize or criminalize same-sex orientation or gender nonconformity, and providing healthy social and recreational outlets for LGBT youth.

Chapter 5 discusses the management of sensitive client information related to LGBT youth. The authors recommend specific steps that agencies can take to create a safe space for LGBT youth to self-identify and selectively share their sexual orientation or gender identity with others ("come out"), while protecting the confidentiality of information regarding sexual orientation or gender identity.

Chapter 6 discusses strategies for ensuring appropriate homes for LGBT youth in care by making individualized placement decisions and recruiting and supporting competent, committed caregivers.

Chapter 7 discusses strategies for ensuring the safety and well-being of LGBT youth in institutional settings by making sound classification and housing decisions, addressing the specific risks to transgender youth, and employing programmatic safety measures.

Chapter 8 addresses the obligation of child welfare and juvenile justice agencies to provide inclusive and nondiscriminatory health and mental health as well as educational services to LGBT youth in their custody.

CHAPTER 1

LGBT Youth in Out-of-Home Care

On any given day, more than half a million children and youth nationally are living away from their families and in the custody of foster care or juvenile justice systems. Quantifying the number of LGBT youth in out-of-home care is difficult because many of these youth hide their sexual orientation and gender identity from adults and peers whom they perceive as rejecting or unsupportive. Research has shown that these fears are well-founded. In a survey of 400 homeless LGBT youth in San Diego, for example, 74% of youth surveyed believed they had received prejudicial treatment, including harassment or threats, after disclosing their sexual or gender identity to providers (Berberet, 2004).

Although there are no reliable statistics, providers and other individuals who work in child welfare and juvenile justice systems consistently report that LGBT youth are disproportionately represented among youth in out-of-home care (CWLA & Lambda Legal, 2006). This chapter discusses the process by which LGBT youth become aware of their sexual orientation or gender identity, the experiences and social conditions that lead to or deepen their involvement in child welfare and juvenile justice systems, and the mistreatment and discrimination people subject them to in out-of-home care.

Self-Awareness of Sexual Orientation and Gender Identity

Sexual orientation is an enduring emotional, romantic, sexual, and affectional attraction to others that is shaped at an early age (American Psychological Association, n.d.). Although there are many theories about the origin of sexual orientation, most scientists agree that it is probably the result of a complex interaction of environmental, cognitive, and biological factors. Sexual orientation exists on a continuum from exclusively homosexual (attraction to same-sex people) to exclusively heterosexual (attraction to opposite-sex people), and includes varied expressions of bisexuality (attraction to same-sex and opposite-sex people).

Many youth realize that they are lesbian, gay, or bisexual long before they become sexually active, some by age 5 (Ryan & Diaz, 2005). Contrary to common misconceptions, adolescents do not need to have a sexual relationship with an opposite-sex (or same-sex) partner to understand their sexual orientation. Likewise, many young people do not identify themselves as lesbian or gay even though they are attracted to people of the same gender. Moreover, no reliable method of determining whether a young person is lesbian, gay, or bisexual simply from his or her appearance or behavior exists.

Gender identity is distinct from sexual orientation and refers to a person's internal identification or self-image as male or female (Kessler & McKenna, 1978; Money, 1973). Every person has a gender identity. Most people's gender identity—their understanding of themselves as male or female—is consistent with their anatomical sex. For a transgender person, however, there is a conflict between the two; the individual's internal identification as male or female differs from his or her anatomical sex (Cole, Emory, Huang, & Meyer, 1994). Gender identity is also established at an early age, generally by age 3.

Gender roles or *sex roles* are social and cultural expectations and beliefs about appropriate male or female behavior. Children generally internalize expectations related to gender roles between ages 3 and 7. Adults often expect children to adhere to culturally defined gender roles and may subtly or overtly sanction children who exhibit behavior contrary to these expectations.

Increasingly, young people who identify as transgender do so during adolescence. Many youth who later identify as transgender report feeling that they were in the wrong body as a young child. This incongruence may cause significant distress, particularly when adults do not understand the child's concerns and try to force the child to comply with the cultural expectations associated with his or her birth gender. Children who understand that the gender messages they get from parents or adults are different from what they feel internally learn to hide these feelings to avoid disapproval or punitive reactions from adults.

Some lesbian, gay, and bisexual individuals exhibit gender-nonconforming behaviors, whereas others fully conform to cultural and social expectations of masculinity and femininity. Regardless of their sexual orientation or gender identity, however, youth who are visibly gender nonconforming are often perceived to be gay or lesbian. Thus, gender nonconformity may fuel anti-gay harassment and abuse, even when the victims are heterosexual. For example, among 8% of students who were harassed and victimized in school because they were perceived to be gay in the Seattle Teen Health Survey (Reis & Saewyc, 1999), 6% were heterosexual. Regardless of their sexual orientation, youth who were victimized because others thought they were gay had the same serious negative outcomes, including significantly higher rates of attempted suicide.

Pathways of LGBT Youth into State Care

LGBT adolescents have the same needs for support, acceptance, and validation from peers, family members, and adults as all young people. These adolescents, however, must also cope with the additional challenge of social stigma related to their sexual orientation or gender identity. For many LGBT youth, victimization in school, home, and community settings is the norm. In addition, most LGBT youth are raised by heterosexual parents or caregivers who lack basic information about LGBT issues. Unlike many of their heterosexual peers, LGBT youth often lack support systems or adult mentors to emulate. Thus, they struggle with their emerging sexual orientation or gender identity—and with anti-LGBT bias—alone, without family or peer support.

LGBT youth enter the child welfare or juvenile justice system for many reasons, many of which are unrelated to their sexual orientation or gender identity. Some are placed in foster care as infants or young children and discover or disclose their sexual orientation or gender identity while in care. Others come from dysfunctional families or from backgrounds that are characterized by abuse and neglect, and caseworkers removed them from their homes for their safety and well-being. Still others have been charged with illegal conduct, such as drug use or truancy, that seems, at least initially, to be unrelated to their sexual orientation or gender identity. A large proportion of LGBT youth enter these systems, however, for reasons either directly or indirectly related to their sexual orientation or gender identity. This includes youth who, because of their sexual orientation or gender identity, have been rejected, neglected, or abused by their birthfamilies; youth who have stopped attending school because of anti-LGBT abuse or harassment; runaway, "throwaway," and homeless youth, some of whom engage in survival crimes; and youth who have been mislabeled as sex offenders simply because of their sexual orientation or gender identity.

A high proportion of LGBT youth who end up in state care leave home or are ejected from their homes as a result of conflict related to their sexual orientation or gender identity. Nearly half (42%) of LGBT youth in out-of-home settings who participated in a study on family acceptance and rejection of LGBT adolescents were either removed or ejected from their homes because of conflict related to their LGBT identity (Ryan & Diaz, 2005). Agencies placed one-third (33%) in foster care or juvenile justice facilities because of behavioral disorders, drugs, or family violence, whereas the others entered care because of parental dysfunction, abuse, and neglect.

As one 16-year-old gay foster youth who participated in a focus group to develop these guidelines explained:

> I ran away a lot because my parents didn't like that I was gay. One time I had a physical fight with my dad and ended up in juvenile hall. Finally, I was kicked out for good and put into foster care.

Others enter state care as status offenders due to chronic truancy because they are afraid to go to school. A national survey of LGBT youth in high schools and middle schools in 48 states found that one in three reported being harassed as a result of his or her sexual orientation, and an equal proportion said they had been harassed because of their gender expression (Kosciw & Cullen, 2001). Most youth (85%) reported hearing homophobic remarks from other students, whereas nearly one-fourth (24%) heard such remarks from faculty or school staff, and few faculty intervened to help. Population-based studies show that lesbian, gay, and bisexual students are more likely to be in a physical fight, to be threatened or injured with a weapon at school, and to skip school because they felt unsafe, compared with their heterosexual peers (Garafalo, Wolf, Kessel, Palfrey, & DuRant, 1998).

Connection to school is an important protective factor that helps prevent health risks and provides a critical context for adolescent development. Youth who are targeted because of their known or perceived sexual orientation, however, reported less connection to school, community, or supportive adults; less support from teachers, family, and friends; and fewer resources for coping with problems than students who are not the targets of anti-gay harassment (California Safe Schools Coalition, 2004).

LGBT youth who are victimized in school are also at risk of school failure and dropping out of school, which significantly affects their prospects for a successful transition to adulthood. The more open youth are about their sexual orientation and the more gender atypical, the more likely they are to be victimized (D'Augelli, Pilkington, & Hershberger, 2002).

Because harassment and victimization are so widespread, many LGBT youth prefer to live on the streets rather than in places in which the adults responsible for their care ignore or tolerate their victimization. A study of lesbian and gay youth in New York City's child welfare system found that more than half (56%) of the youth interviewed said they stayed on the streets at times because they felt safer there than living in group or foster homes (Mallon, 1998). Among LGBT homeless youth in San Diego, 39% said they were ejected from their home or placements because of their sexual orientation (Berberet, 2004).

Homelessness exposes LGBT youth to a host of other problems, including involvement in criminal activity (prostitution, theft, drug sales) and increased risk of victimization (assault, robbery, rape). Homeless LGBT youth often engage in survival sex, which puts them at risk for incarceration, HIV infection, and violence. Among high-risk homeless youth, LGBT homeless youth report the highest rates of victimization, risk, and health concerns (Cochran, Stewart, Joshua, Ginzler, & Cauce, 2002).

Some LGBT youth enter state care after they are arrested and charged with a sex offense for engaging in consensual conduct or relationships with same-sex partners that would not result in arrest or prosecution if the youth involved were of the opposite sex. Often, the impetus for filing formal charges comes from a parent who finds same-sex encounters abhorrent and insists on characterizing his or her child as a victim rather than a willing participant. In other cases, school or group care facility staff who discover youth in same-sex relationships may feel obligated to identify a perpetrator or scapegoat and to press criminal charges. Designation as a sex offender can have lifelong negative legal consequences, including registration requirements, exclusion from employment or volunteer work in jobs involving children, and denial of legal residency or citizenship status.

Family rejection, school victimization, homelessness, and improper criminal charges are all expressions of societal bias and stigma. Any of these conditions can contribute to the involvement of LGBT youth in child welfare or juvenile justice systems. Cumulatively, these conditions deepen and unnecessarily prolong the involvement of LGBT youth in child welfare and juvenile justice systems and contribute to the disproportionate numbers of LGBT youth in out-of-home care.

Mistreatment of LGBT Youth in Out-of-Home Care

The rejection, harassment, and discrimination directed at LGBT youth by their peers, families, and communities often continues or worsens in foster care and juvenile justice settings. LGBT youth commonly experience multiple and frequent placement changes prompted by overt discrimination or harassment from peers, caregivers, and staff. One study found that 78% of LGBT youth were removed or ran away from their placements as a result of hostility toward their sexual orientation or gender identity (Joint Task Force, 1994). Many LGBT youth run away from placements in which they have experienced ongoing discrimination, harassment, or violence, including sexual assault. For example, among homeless LGBT youth in San Diego, 64% of youth who were interviewed reported having had prior residential placements (Berberet, 2004). One of the lesbian youth from the focus groups reported that the staff in her group home regularly called lesbian youth names and told them that they were going to hell. This treatment made it intolerable for her to live in the group home, and so she ran away.

LGBT youth in juvenile justice facilities also face persistent anti-gay harassment and physical assault. Many youth report sexual assault by staff and other youth in these facilities. In focus groups conducted for these guidelines, all youth who participated reported having experienced verbal harassment in juvenile justice facilities on a regular basis. As one gay youth explained, "I was really unsafe, especially in the showers." Another youth was sexually assaulted by a staff member in a juvenile detention facility. He explained, "During the investigation I took a polygraph test, and it supported what I told them, but they still said my allegations were false, and they did nothing."

In many juvenile detention and correctional facilities, LGBT youth who were not accused or convicted of a sex offense are housed in sex-offender units. In these facilities, having a lesbian, gay, or bisexual identity or identifying as transgender often is wrongly perceived as being synonymous with having a "sexual issue" or "sexual problem" among staff with a limited understanding of human sexuality. These practices are both unconstitutional[9] and extremely harmful. For a young person who has not engaged in

---

[9]   Courts have found that the classification of an adult inmate as a sex offender has such stigmatizing consequences that unless the inmate has a sexual-offense history, additional constitutional requirements must be met before institutions can assign this classification. See *Neal v. Shimoda* (1997): "We can hardly conceive of a state's action bearing more 'stigmatizing consequences' than the labeling of a prison inmate as a sex offender."

any improper or inappropriate conduct, being labeled and treated as a sex offender is devastating and may cause permanent psychological damage.

Many LGBT youth report that when they turn to adults in the system for protection from abuse, the adults either ignore them or blame them for being victimized. A gay youth from one of the focus groups was sexually and physically assaulted on numerous occasions while in a detention facility, eventually resulting in a gang rape. Although he reported these incidents, the staff took no actions to protect him. He explained:

> The staff think that if a youth is gay, they want to have sex with all of the other boys. It's not true! And they would not help me when the other youth abused me and forced me to have sex.

A transgender youth from the focus groups was repeatedly beaten by boys in her group home. The youth reported the abuse to her social worker, but rather than helping her, the social worker said, "It's your fault. Stop acting like a girl."

Even when staff members are well-meaning, they often lack the knowledge or training to provide appropriate services to LGBT youth. For example, staff members frequently respond to the harassment or assault of an LGBT youth by isolating or moving the LGBT youth—often to a more restrictive facility—rather than addressing the underlying prejudice. Although this response may make it easier to protect the young person, it punishes the victim and often results in drastically reduced services and psychological distress for LGBT youth. It is also a violation of the LGBT youth's constitutional rights.[10]

Staff members may also segregate or isolate LGBT youth based on the erroneous assumption that LGBT youth will prey on other wards. One of the lesbian youth interviewed for these guidelines explained that she was not allowed to have a roommate or to spend unsupervised time with other girls. This segregation made her feel that something was wrong with her. She explained, "Just because I'm like this doesn't mean you have to cordon me off from everybody else." Another gay youth described being forced to spend time in lockdown and on suicide watch, although he was not a

---

[10] For example, in *R.G. v. Koller* (2006), the Hawaii Youth Correctional Facility (HYCF) admitted that staff used isolation as a means of protecting wards who were known or perceived to be LGBT. The court found this practice to be both harmful and punitive, explaining, "Consistently placing juvenile wards in isolation...simply to separate LGBT wards from their abusers, cannot be viewed in any reasonable light as advancing a legitimate nonpunitive governmental objective. HYCF has attempted to remedy one harm with an indefensible and unconstitutional solution."

discipline problem or a suicide risk, based on a presumption that he could not be trusted around other youth simply because he was gay. In addition, even youth who are not segregated or placed in increased security settings often are not allowed access to LGBT-supportive programs such as youth groups, LGBT centers, or other LGBT social activities because staff do not understand why these services are important or because they think it is inappropriate or morally wrong to support a young person's sexual orientation or gender identity.

Not all of the experiences of LGBT youth in out-of-home care are negative. Some youth in care recall supportive adults who treated them respectfully and provided support. Such caring relationships are critical factors in promoting resilience and helping youth deal with adversity (Benard, 2004). One youth noted the positive effect of having an openly gay counselor, who believed the youth when he reported being assaulted: "This counselor was the only person I could talk to about everything because he was not judgmental, and he was understanding of these issues." Another youth found support from a mentor in a youth community program. The mentor created a safe, trusting relationship that enabled the youth to talk about feelings related to his identity. These positive experiences underscore the importance and positive effect on LGBT youth of providing respectful, sensitive care, the rudiments of quality care for all young people, regardless of sexual orientation, gender, ethnicity, or personal background.

CHAPTER 2

Creating an Inclusive Organizational Culture

The most critical aspect of improving services to LGBT youth in public custody is creating an organizational culture in which the inherent worth and dignity of every person is respected and every person is treated fairly and equally. An inclusive and respectful environment benefits all youth by making it safe for young people to explore their own emerging identities—a crucial developmental task for adolescents—and to accept and value differences in others.

This is particularly important for LGBT adolescents, who often have internalized negative attitudes and distorted stereotypes about a core aspect of their identity. To develop a healthy, integrated identity, these adolescents must transform a negative identity into a positive one and learn to manage stigma—a challenging task regardless of age or developmental level. Creating an environment in which LGBT youth feel safe exploring and disclosing their emerging identities promotes well-being, helps build self-esteem, and helps adolescents learn self-care, an essential component in reducing risk and promoting healthy behaviors. In turn, creating an environment in which youth can be open about their developing identities provides agency personnel and caregivers with information that is essential to developing appropriate and individualized services.

Creating and supporting an inclusive organizational culture requires a comprehensive approach based on core values that are consistently reinforced. Although nondiscrimination policies are the cornerstone of organizational change, agencies cannot achieve inclusiveness by mechanically adopting polices and procedures. Rather, agency leadership must authentically understand and convey the value of inclusiveness and reinforce this message at all levels of the organization. Every employee, contractor, service provider, caregiver, family member, and young person involved in the system should know and understand the agency's commitment to treating every person with respect, valuing and affirming differences, and preventing harassment or discrimination of any kind.

This chapter outlines concrete steps that child welfare and juvenile justice agencies can take to create an inclusive organizational culture, including:

- adopting and enforcing a nondiscrimination policy and grievance procedure, as well as

- providing training for agency personnel, contractors, direct care staff, and caregivers on how to implement the nondiscrimination policy.

Adopting Written Nondiscrimination Policies

Often, both youth and adults in the system practice and tolerate discrimination and harassment based on sexual orientation and gender identity. To demonstrate their commitment to ending this practice, child welfare and juvenile justice agencies should adopt written policies prohibiting harassment and discrimination on the basis of actual or perceived sexual orientation or gender identity. Adopting a nondiscrimination policy that explicitly includes sexual orientation and gender identity makes clear that anti-LGBT harassment and discrimination is unacceptable behavior that will not be tolerated. The existence of such a policy also gives staff members the support they need to respond appropriately to anti-LGBT harassment. The policy should:

- prohibit all forms of harassment and discrimination, including jokes, slurs, and name calling;

- apply to all agency personnel from managers to caseworkers, providers who contract to serve youth in the agency's custody, and all direct care staff, including foster parents, relative caregivers, and facility staff;

- protect agency personnel and contractors, as well as youth and families served by the agency; and

- include a formal grievance procedure that allows for confidential complaints and neutral third-party investigations.

Adopting and enforcing a policy that prohibits violence, name calling, and other harassment or discrimination promotes equitable care for all young people. Such a policy does not infringe on individual beliefs about homosexuality or gender roles. Providers and staff members are free to hold any beliefs they choose, so long as they enforce and adhere to the agency's nondiscrimination policy.

Agencies should ensure that all youth, families, providers, staff, and caregivers are aware of the agency's nondiscrimination policy by:

- including a copy of the policy in the staff training or orientation for every new employee, contractor, and caregiver;

- discussing application of the policy to help employees and caregivers understand what it means to provide nondiscriminatory treatment and services;

- including the policy in any written handbook or orientation materials provided to youth entering the system;

- discussing the policy with every child who is capable of understanding it;

- posting the policy in agency offices, group care facilities, courtrooms, and other strategic locations; and

- including the policy in culturally and developmentally appropriate written materials designed for youth and their families.

Effective implementation of a nondiscrimination policy requires a written procedure for filing and resolving complaints of discrimination or harassment. To evaluate implementation and performance of nondiscrimination policies, agencies should keep records of each complaint and its resolution. It is also helpful to appoint an oversight body or individual to review the grievance records regularly to identify potential problems, patterns, or need for additional training.

Providing Training on the Application of the Nondiscrimination Policy

To effectively implement a nondiscrimination policy, child welfare and juvenile justice agencies must provide initial and ongoing professional training to all agency personnel (including administrators, managers, supervisors, and line staff), as well as group care staff, licensing personnel, relative and foster family caregivers, and health and mental health providers with whom the agency contracts. Training is a crucial aspect of creating cultural change in agencies because it reinforces the agency's commitment to providing appropriate and inclusive care, and it replaces common myths and misconceptions with practical, research-based information regarding LGBT youth. It is not enough for agencies to commit to providing appropriate care to LGBT youth;

they must provide the tools and support to make this commitment a reality. Agencies should obtain or develop a training curriculum that covers the following topics:

- A review of vocabulary and definitions relevant to LGBT youth
- An exploration of myths and stereotypes regarding LGBT youth and adults
- Developmental issues and adaptive strategies for LGBT children and youth
- Promoting positive development of LGBT children and adolescents
- A review of the coming-out process and how families and adults can support a young person who is coming out
- A discussion of how sexual orientation or gender identity may relate to the reasons a young person is in state custody
- The issues and challenges unique to transgender youth
- Approaches to working with the families of LGBT youth
- Guidance on how to serve LGBT youth respectfully and equitably
- Agency and community resources available to serve LGBT youth and their families

Trainers should engage participants in open discussions and encourage them to ask questions. The training should emphasize practical solutions and provide concrete suggestions for creating LGBT-affirming environments. These suggestions might include:

- Adopting and enforcing a policy prohibiting the use of slurs or jokes based on race, culture, gender, gender identity, sexual orientation, or any other individual difference
- Displaying "hate-free zone" posters or other symbols indicating an LGBT-friendly environment (rainbow flags, pink triangles, etc.)
- Including LGBT-affirming books, magazines, and videos in agency libraries
- Openly reaching out to the LGBT community to recruit agency personnel, facility staff, mentors, and foster and adoptive families

- Using respectful and inclusive terminology that does not make assumptions about another individual's sexual orientation or gender identity
- Creating opportunities for dialogue with youth and staff about all forms of diversity, including sexual orientation and gender identity
- Promptly and consistently intervening when youth or adults behave disrespectfully toward an individual or group based on sexual orientation, gender identity, or other differences
- Treating youth and adults with equanimity and avoiding double standards

CHAPTER 3

A Family-Centered Approach to Serving LGBT Youth

All youth need and deserve families to nurture them and help them make a successful transition to adulthood. Research has documented the negative outcomes for youth and young adults who are disconnected from their families and other forms of social support (Wald & Martinez, 2003). The prospects for youth who exit state custody with no permanent family connections are particularly dire. These youth face significant risk of homelessness, poverty, incarceration, and victimization (North American Council on Adoptable Children, 2005).

Family support is especially crucial for LGBT youth, who must navigate the usual challenges associated with adolescence while learning to manage a stigmatized identity and cope with social, educational, and community environments in which victimization and harassment are the norm. Supportive families help LGBT youth develop the self-confidence and resilience necessary to integrate positive and healthy identities in a pre-dominantly hostile environment. Conversely, family rejection places LGBT youth at high risk for abuse, neglect, and self-destructive or antisocial behaviors, which can lead to out-of-home placement and negative health and mental health outcomes.

Despite the importance of family support to promote the health and well-being of LGBT youth, most programs and providers serve them as individuals rather than members of families and communities (Mallon, 1999b; Ryan & Futterman, 1997). This chapter proposes that child welfare and juvenile justice agencies develop services that strengthen and support the families of LGBT youth while protecting the youths' safety and addressing any negative or self-destructive behaviors. First, the authors discuss the societal changes and challenges confronting contemporary LGBT youth and their families, and their need for information and sup-port. Next, they describe the steps that child welfare and juvenile justice agencies can take to increase family communication and understanding, decrease family rejection, and repair and preserve family connections.

Finally, they describe the steps child welfare and juvenile justice agencies can take to create and support permanent connections for LGBT youth who cannot reconcile with their families.

Contemporary LGBT Youth and Their Families

LGBT children are self-identifying and coming out to their families and others at increasingly younger ages. An analysis of research conducted with lesbian and gay adults in the 1970s showed that the average age they reported being aware of same-sex attraction was between 14 and 16, and the average age they self-identified as gay or lesbian was between 19 and 23 (Troiden, 1988). By comparison, a review of studies on lesbian, gay, and bisexual adolescents from the late 1980s and early 1990s shows that the average age that children were first aware of same-sex attraction was between 9 and 10, and the average age at which lesbian and gay youth self-identified was between 14 and 16 (Ryan & Futterman, 1997, 2001). In a current study of LGBT adolescents, the average age of same-sex attraction is about 10, but lesbian and gay adolescents are self-identifying, on average, at age 13.4, and several self-identified at ages 5 to 7 (Ryan & Diaz, 2005). Although comparable information is not available for transgender youth, many adolescents initially identify as lesbian or gay before they identify as transgender, which in the same study occurred at ages 13 to 16 (Ryan & Diaz, 2005).

Several factors are responsible for these changes, including increased access to information about human sexuality and gender identity in general. Increased visibility and positive representations of LGBT individuals in the media and popular culture have helped young people understand their feelings and put them in a social context. Enhanced visibility and social acceptance of LGBT individuals is a positive change that supports healthy adolescent development. These societal changes, however, have also created new challenges for the families of LGBT youth, which in turn necessitate new approaches to serving these youth and their families.

Thirty years ago, families generally learned of their children's LGBT status after the child had become an adult and left home. Many parents struggled with coming to terms with their child's LGBT identity, and these conflicts sometimes caused permanent and painful family ruptures. Even when parents disowned or rejected their adult children, however, their reactions remained a private matter. Young LGBT adults and their families resolved, or failed to resolve, these issues on their own terms—often gradually and over a period of years.

By contrast, contemporary families typically confront these issues while their children are much younger—usually living at home and under their parents' direct supervision. Parents often have particular difficulty accepting their child's emerging LGBT identity when the child is an adolescent or preadolescent for whom they are responsible and over whom they expect to have ongoing influence. Many parents view their adolescent or preadolescent child's expression or exploration of sexuality as premature and dangerous, and they believe it is their responsibility to suppress or delay the child's sexuality—whatever form it takes. The parent's distress is exacerbated when the child explores or claims a sexual identity that the parent views as deviant or morally repugnant.

Moreover, when their LGBT child is a minor, parental rejection has significant implications. Children under the age of majority are legally, emotionally, and practically dependent on the care and support of their families. Younger children are more vulnerable and dependent on family support. Parental rejection is more likely to subject a younger child to significant psychological injury. Extreme parental rejection of a minor child—such as severe emotional abuse, physical abuse, or ejection from the home—may also set in motion the conditions triggering state intervention.

Researchers from the Family Acceptance Project—the first major study of LGBT adolescents and their families—have documented the significance of family responses to children's emerging LGBT identities on the young people's health and mental health (Ryan & Diaz, 2005). Ryan and Diaz (2005) found that family and caregiver acceptance is an important protective factor, and family and caregiver rejection has serious negative health outcomes for LGBT youth. LGBT young people whose families and caregivers rejected their sexual orientation during adolescence were much more likely to report higher rates of depression, suicidality, substance abuse problems, and risk for HIV infection than their peers who reported having families and caregivers who had accepted their sexual identity. Family acceptance and rejection also affected self-esteem, access to social support, and life satisfaction.

The stories of family members who participated in the Family Acceptance Project clearly demonstrate the challenges faced by LGBT youth and their families, as well as their need for support and information. Across ethnic, socioeconomic, and geographic lines, the study participants reported similar experiences. Regardless of their beliefs and backgrounds, most families in the study struggled to adapt to their children's sexual orientation or gender identity. Some parents could not reconcile their child's sexual orientation or gender identity with their own strongly held religious beliefs or moral views.

Virtually all families—including those who were overtly rejecting—also reported concern for their child's safety and well-being. They expressed an urgent need for information and contact with other families experiencing similar issues, fear for their child's safety, and a desire to resolve family conflict related to their child's LGBT identity. Unfortunately, most families struggled in isolation, without community resources such as access to knowledgeable providers or support groups, to help them learn about and adjust to their child's sexual orientation or gender identity. These findings validate the need for family-centered interventions designed to help families come to terms with their children's sexual orientation or gender identity (Ryan & Diaz, 2005). The Family Acceptance Project is working on developing a new model of family-related care to help strengthen families and increase support for LGBT youth while helping maintain these adolescents in their homes.

Supporting Family Acceptance and Reconciliation

Research from the Family Acceptance Project shows that many families become less rejecting and more accepting within about two years of learning about their child's LGBT identity (Ryan & Diaz, 2005).This timeframe does not meet the needs of LGBT youth who may sustain irreparable emotional injury while their families make this adjustment. Fortunately, the research also demonstrates that intervention by knowledgeable providers who are trained to assess family dynamics, provide counseling and accurate information, and educate families about the effect of their words, actions, and behaviors on their child's well-being can make a substantial difference in helping families adjust more rapidly. These interventions can help increase the level of communication and understanding, decrease family rejection, prevent unnecessary family disruption, and ultimately, improve the child's health and mental health outcomes (Ryan & Diaz, 2005).

Child welfare and juvenile justice agencies should provide a range of family-centered services to LGBT youth and their families, including prevention services, intensive home-based services, educational services, and reunification services.

Prevention Services

Child welfare and juvenile justice agencies, in conjunction with other public systems serving children, youth, and families, should partner with appropriate community-based organizations to provide free, accessible information and support to youth and families who want to learn more about sexual orientation and gender identity. The Family Acceptance Project is currently developing evidence-based family education materials to help families and caregivers adjust to their child's nonheterosexual identity (see http://familyproject.sfsu.edu). Access to information and support may prevent or minimize family conflict or crisis by helping youth and families understand and anticipate the coming-out process and the family's adjustment to it. Findings from the Family Acceptance Project indicate that early intervention to help families and caregivers understand the effect of their reactions to their child's LGBT identity can help maintain many LGBT youth in their homes. These services may also prevent the need for more formal or intensive interventions. Ideally, youth or families should be able to access prevention services independently and confidentially. The services also must be accessible practically, linguistically, and culturally. Placing these services in a community setting, rather than a government agency, will likely enhance their accessibility.

Intensive Home-Based Services

Child welfare and juvenile justice systems should develop intensive home-based services to respond to the immediate crisis precipitated by the family's discovery of a child's sexual orientation or gender identity. These systems should regard family crisis as an important opportunity to strengthen families and increase support for LGBT children and adolescents (Mallon, 1998; Ryan & Diaz, 2005). Families in crisis are more amenable to change because of the need to relieve immediate distress and restore family equilibrium.

Agencies should provide immediate, intensive, home-based services to stabilize the family and maintain the LGBT youth in the home if possible. These services should include:

- support, counseling, and guidance in coping with the immediate adjustment to family's discovery of the youth's sexual orientation or gender identity;

- information and guidance related to positive adolescent development, human sexuality and gender identity, and the effects on the youth of family acceptance or rejection;

- individual and family counseling to support each family member and improve family communication and functioning; and

- assistance identifying local services and resources to provide ongoing support to the family and the youth.

To effectively intervene, home-based practitioners must be familiar with the experiences of LGBT youth and their families, particularly with respect to the coming-out process. Practitioners should also be trained to assess family dynamics and ensure the physical and emotional safety of the young person.

Educational Services

Families need accurate information to help them understand their child's experience and the effect of their behavior on their child's well-being. Parents and other family members may ascribe to myths or misconceptions about sexual orientation or gender identity that make their and their child's adjustments much more difficult. Some families believe that gay and lesbian individuals present a threat to young children and may prevent LGBT youth from having contact with younger siblings or relatives. Others believe that therapy or other interventions can reverse or change their child's emerging sexual orientation or gender identity. Still others believe that their child is doomed to a life of loneliness and isolation. Even relatively accepting families often believe that they may have somehow caused their child to become lesbian, gay, bisexual, or transgender. Practitioners can debunk these stereotypes by discussing these issues with parents, providing them access to reading material or relevant Internet sites, or referring them to support groups or counseling services. Families can also serve as a resource for one another, providing an informal and nonthreatening opportunity to share experiences and support.

Researchers from the Family Acceptance Project found that families desperately needed help understanding how they could maintain a place in the family for their child, particularly if they were struggling with strongly held religious or moral beliefs. Family members need validation for their feelings and guidance in understanding how their words and actions affect their child's well-being. When an adolescent comes out or when families find out that their child identifies as lesbian, gay, bisexual, or transgender, families need to know that they can ultimately find a way to incorporate their child into family life while still maintaining their values and beliefs, and this adjustment will take time, education, and communication. For many families and adolescents, religion and spirituality are important sources of coping and strength, and providers need to help them understand that loving their child and finding solace in their beliefs are not mutually exclusive (Ryan & Diaz, 2005).

Reunification Services

Agencies should invest primarily in strategies designed to support the attachments of LGBT youth to their extended families. Some families, however, will not be capable of meeting the youth's safety needs—even with intensive support. Thus, agencies must be able to assess the family's capacity to adjust and ensure the youth's immediate emotional and physical safety. In some cases, it will still be necessary to provide substitute care, at least for some period of time. Under these circumstances, agencies should continue to work with families that have the capacity, with support and education, to strengthen their relationships and to reintegrate their child into family life, with the goal of reunifying young people with their families, whenever possible. While they are in state custody, youth should have ongoing contact with their families, including their siblings, consistent with their safety and their stated wishes.

Permanent Connections for LGBT Youth

For some LGBT youth, family preservation or reconciliation is not a viable option. Some families are unwilling or unable to provide a safe and stable home for their lesbian, gay, bisexual, or transgender child. Many of the young people from these families will exit systems of care without the support and social connections essential to their long-term well-being. Several studies have documented the bleak futures and high risk (Ryan & Diaz, 2005) of these disconnected youth (e.g., Wald & Martinez, 2003). In particular, the lack of consistent, supportive relationships with adults places youth at a significant disadvantage psychologically, economically, and socially (Hair, Jager, & Garrett, 2002).

Acknowledging these realities, child welfare practice has shifted away from long-term foster care and independent-living services to reunification, adoption, and legal guardianship to provide youth with permanent family connections. To address the complexity and diversity of young people's lives, some experts have broadened the concept of permanence to encompass arrangements other than reunification and adoption that create lifelong connections to caring, committed adults. For example, the California Permanency for Youth Project defines *permanence* as:

> both a process and a result that includes involvement of the youth as a participant or leader in finding a permanent connection with at least one committed adult who provides: a safe, stable and secure parenting relationship, love, unconditional commitment, and lifelong support in the context of reunification, legal adoption or guardianship, where possible, and in which the youth has the opportunity to maintain contacts with important persons including brothers and sisters. (Louisell, 2004)

Although the concept of permanence is generally associated with child welfare practice, the benefits of permanent connections apply equally to delinquent youth. In fact, youth involved in the juvenile justice system may be at even greater risk for disconnection from family and social supports. Most of these youth exit the system with no aftercare or transitional services and no effort to ensure their connection to appropriate supports in their families and communities.

LGBT youth, like all youth, need permanent connections to committed, supportive adults. Unfortunately, however, these youth face additional obstacles to achieving permanence, and they often lack permanent connections to their communities and birthfamilies (Jacobs & Freundlich, 2006). Because of the shortage of LGBT-affirming family placements, a disproportionate percentage of LGBT youth in out-of-home care are placed in congregate care. Studies have shown that youth in congregate care are significantly less likely than youth in family settings to achieve permanence (Freundlich & Avery, 2005; U.S. Department of Health and Human Services, 2003). Multiple, unstable placements stemming from a lack of acceptance of the youth or overt discrimination directed at them also undermine permanence for LGBT youth (Mallon, Aledort, & Ferrera, 2002). Older youth in general, and LGBT teens specifically, are less likely to have family-based permanency plans. Finally, having experienced multiple rejections, LGBT youth may have difficulty trusting and depending on adults and may resist permanence.

Child welfare agencies can use several strategies to meet the permanency needs of LGBT youth, including developing a strong agency focus on permanence for LGBT youth; working closely with LGBT youth to create workable, individualized permanency plans; reducing the agency's reliance on group care for LGBT youth; and providing training and ongoing support to families and adults who make permanent commitments to LGBT youth.

Developing a Strong Agency Focus on Permanence

One important step in meeting the permanency needs of LGBT youth is to build agency support for concept that LGBT youth need and deserve permanent, loving families, and that some families are willing to make this commitment (Jacobs & Freundlich, 2006). To this end, agencies should develop guidelines and procedures to support permanency plans for all LGBT youth. These guidelines and policies should limit the use of independent living as a case goal, limit the use of congregate care, develop a youth-driven permanency model, and train all staff in general permanency strategies as well as overcoming the barriers to permanence experienced by LGBT youth (Jacobs & Freundlich, 2006; North American Council on Adoptable Children [NACAC], 2005).

Working Closely with LGBT Youth

LGBT youth are an invaluable resource in developing their own permanency plans. Many creative new programs use specially trained social workers to work closely with youth to identify adults with whom they have an existing connection and who could be a permanent resource for the youth (Louisell, 2004). These programs use specific strategies to closely review the youth's case record and to assist the young person in identifying important adult relationships in his or her life. These strategies are particularly useful for LGBT youth, who are crucial players in identifying LGBT-affirming adults and families with whom they have existing connections.

Youth-driven identification of potential permanent families is also consistent with a broader and more flexible conception of permanence and provides more permanency options for LGBT youth. In one study of LGBT youth in foster care, youth identified fictive kin (unrelated adults whom the youth views as family), agency staff members, and adult role models and mentors as potential permanency resources (Mallon et al., 2002). When reunification and adoption are not viable options, a more flexible approach also permits LGBT youth to work with the agency to develop other types of permanent arrangements. Youth most often prioritize relational permanence (a permanent relationship with an adult) and physical permanence (a place to live) over legal permanence (adoption or guardianship; Sanchez, 2004).

Working closely with youth also provides an opportunity to address their fears or concerns about permanence (Jacobs & Freundlich, 2006). Having been subjected to repeated rejection, many LGBT youth fear that they will never be accepted. Youth who have lived on the streets with little or no adult supervision for any length of time may have difficulty imagining being part of a family. LGBT youth who have internalized societal biases may feel unworthy of having a family. Many LGBT youth have unresolved issues with their birthfamilies and may be reluctant to commit to another adult or family. Enlisting the active participation of LGBT youth in creating their permanency plans may help them overcome a feeling of powerlessness by making them agents of change in their own lives.

Reducing Reliance on Group Care for LGBT Youth

Because of a real or perceived shortage of LGBT-affirming family resources, agencies disproportionately place LGBT youth in congregate care settings. Many of the LGBT youth placed in group care do not require the additional structure and institutional supports provided by group care. Moreover, residents of group care facilities are much less likely to transition to family settings and are much more likely to run away or age out of systems of care (NACAC, 2005). Agencies should challenge the assumption that the only safe placement for LGBT youth is in a residential facility, and they should invest resources in recruiting, training, and supporting LGBT-affirming families. Child welfare and juvenile justice agencies should also create family-centered transition plans for all LGBT youth, including those who are placed in a group care setting.

Providing Training and Ongoing Support to Permanent Families

Permanent placements of older youth are more likely to be successful if families receive initial training and information, as well as ongoing support (NACAC, 2005). Agencies should provide adults and families who make a permanent commitment to LGBT youth with accurate, evidence-based information about LGBT youth, including the effects of social stigma on adolescent development. These families also need to understand the challenges they may confront as they adjust to a permanent relationship and the support their LGBT child will need at home and in the world. Failed permanency plans are devastating for any young person, but they are particularly damaging to youth who have already suffered multiple rejections—like many LGBT youth.

CHAPTER 4

Promoting Positive Adolescent Development

Adolescence is a time of significant cognitive, emotional, and physical development, when young people must learn to master a range of skills and developmental tasks. LGBT youth have the same developmental tasks as their heterosexual and nontransgender peers, but they also face additional challenges in learning to manage a stigmatized identity and to cope with social, educational, and community environments in which victimization and harassment are the norm. Stigma has social, behavioral, and health-related consequences that can increase risk behaviors, such as unprotected sex and substance abuse, and intensify psychological distress and risk for suicide (Ryan & Futterman, 1997).

Coming out during adolescence and disclosing one's sexual orientation or gender identity to others promotes self-esteem and helps decrease these negative outcomes. Youth who share their sexual orientation with others report feeling better about themselves and more comfortable being "out" at school and in their communities (D'Augelli, Hershberger, & Pilkington, 1998), underscoring the importance of providing a safe space in which youth are able to integrate a positive LGBT identity. In practice, however, families, caregivers, and social institutions often denigrate or even punish LGBT youth for these normative developmental strivings.

In this chapter, the authors elaborate on the obligation of child welfare and juvenile justice agencies to support the healthy development of LGBT youth in their care by supporting the integration of their sexual and gender identity, prohibiting practices that pathologize or criminalize same-sex orientation or gender nonconformity, and providing positive social and recreational outlets for LGBT youth.

Supporting the Positive Development and Expression of Sexual Orientation

Exploration, expression, and integration of identity are crucial parts of positive adolescent development. These normal processes are interrupted, sometimes with tragic results, when youth are punished for, or prevented from, exploring or expressing their sexual orientation. Failure to provide lesbian, gay, or bisexual youth with the same developmental opportunities and support as other youth is discriminatory and harms all youth by planting the seeds of bias and fear that may escalate into harassment and violence. Child welfare and juvenile justice agencies should adopt policies and practices that permit youth to:

- disclose their sexual orientation to other youth, caregivers, and agency personnel;

- discuss their feelings of attraction to youth of the same sex, consistent with discussion of romantic attachments among heterosexual youth, without being penalized or shamed;

- participate in social activities that are geared toward or inclusive of lesbian, gay, and bisexual youth;

- express their sexual orientation through their choice of clothing, jewelry, or hairstyle;

- have access to LGBT-inclusive, supportive books and materials; and

- post LGBT-friendly posters or stickers in their rooms.

During adolescence, youth become increasingly aware of their sexuality and romantic interests. Not all youth who self-identify as lesbian, gay, or bisexual are sexually active or involved in same-sex relationships. Like heterosexual youth, most lesbian, gay, and bisexual youth become aware of their sexual orientation based on their thoughts and emotions, often long before they have relationships or engage in any intimate behavior. Likewise, not all youth who have same-sex feelings, experiences, or relationships self-identify as lesbian, gay, or bisexual. Some youth may be exploring their identity. Others may be fearful of negative repercussions if they self-identify or share their sexual identity with others. Still others may simply wish to avoid labeling themselves. Regardless of how a youth self-identifies or how others perceive him or her, child welfare and juvenile justice professionals should treat all youth equally, respectfully, and with sensitivity to the developmental issues faced by all adolescents.

Group homes and other congregate care facilities often adopt rules limiting romantic relationships or prohibiting intimate conduct by youth. These rules should serve legitimate health and safety goals, and agencies should not use them to discriminate against LGBT youth, to punish LGBT youth for conduct that is not prohibited for other youth, or to shame or humiliate any youth for normative adolescent exploration and development.

Caregivers and providers should be careful to ensure that any rules regarding intimate behavior are applied equally to all youth. Agencies should not penalize youth who become romantically involved with a youth of the same sex when the same involvement with a person of a different sex would not result in punishment. Thus, if girls may hold hands or have a romantic relationship with boys, the same conduct between youth of the same sex should also be permitted. Youth in state care who are living in family settings should be permitted to develop age-appropriate relationships with youth of the same sex and should not be punished or ridiculed for doing so.

Supporting the Positive Development and Expression of Gender Identity

The integration of a positive gender identity is also a critical aspect of healthy adolescent development. This task is especially challenging for transgender youth, whose gender identity does not correspond with their anatomical sex. It is also challenging for youth who are not transgender, but who have characteristics, interests, or behaviors that do not conform to gender stereotypes. Whether youth are transgender or merely gender nonconforming, they are often subjected to ridicule and harassment, which may escalate into sexual assault or other forms of violence. These youth need sensitive and informed care and support to develop into healthy adults.

Child welfare and juvenile justice agencies should not require youth to conform to traditional conceptions of gender or punish youth who are transgender or gender nonconforming. The agency's basic approach should be to validate a young person's core gender identity, as defined by the youth. Agency personnel should not require youth to dress, behave, or express themselves in narrowly proscribed ways because of their gender. Thus, agencies should allow boys to express themselves in stereotypically feminine ways and girls to express themselves in stereotypically masculine ways. Caregivers and facility staff should permit transgender youth to wear clothing that is consistent with their gender identity and should not force them to wear clothing according to their birth sex.

Likewise, caregivers and facility staff should avoid unnecessarily segregating activities according to gender, and they should encourage youth to participate in educational and recreational activities that interest them—regardless of whether these activities are considered stereotypically male or female. Agency personnel, caregivers, and staff members should use the name and pronoun preferred by an individual youth, whether or not these conform to the youth's birth sex, and they should require other youth to do the same. Agency files and other documents should also use the youth's preferred name or pronoun.

On occasion, agency staff may encounter a youth whose gender is not easily classifiable. Rather than making an assumption or a guess, agency personnel should ask the young person about his or her gender identity and how he or she prefers to be addressed. A young person may also undergo gender transition while in care. Agency personnel should adhere to the young person's wishes with respect to name and pronoun during this transition period.

Prohibiting Practices That Pathologize, Punish, or Criminalize LGBT Youth

LGBT youth need to feel that they will be safe and will not be condemned, pathologized, or criminalized if they explore and express their sexual orientation or gender identity through normative means of expression that are expected of and appropriate for all youth. These expressions include romantic attachments and discussion of romantic attachments, dress, recreational and social activities, hobbies, and expressions of affection such as kissing or holding hands.

- Agency personnel should not condemn, criticize, or pathologize youth who explore their attractions for same-sex youth in an age-appropriate, consensual manner. Agencies should be particularly vigilant to prohibit any attempt to characterize these youth as predators or sex offenders.

- Agency personnel, facility staff, and caregivers should not subject LGBT youth to lectures, sermons, or other materials that condemn or pathologize homosexuality or gender nonconformity. For example, agencies should prohibit individual staff members or caregivers from telling LGBT youth that they are sinful or "going to hell."

- Agency policies should prohibit the caregivers or providers from forcing youth to undergo reparative therapy in an attempt to cure them of their same-sex attraction or gender nonconformity.

- Agency policies should prohibit the use of isolation or segregation as a means to protect LGBT youth from violence and harassment.

- Agency policies should prohibit staff members or caregivers from blaming LGBT youth when others subject them to discrimination, harassment, or violence.

Permitting or condoning any of these practices sends a message to LGBT youth that they are deviant, immoral, or mentally ill. These practices also violate the legal obligation of child welfare and juvenile justice agencies to ensure the safety of LGBT youth in their care and to treat them fairly and equally.

Providing Positive Social and Recreational Outlets

Agencies should ensure that LGBT youth in their care have access to age-appropriate social, spiritual, and recreational opportunities that encourage and support these youth in developing into self-assured, healthy adults. These opportunities can help provide LGBT youth with emotional support and confidence as they come to understand and accept their sexual and gender identities. Socializing with LGBT peers can help alleviate alienation and isolation by introducing youth to others who share their experiences. LGBT-supportive programming can have a markedly positive effect on the outlook of LGBT youth because these settings embrace LGBT youth for who they are, rather than merely tolerating them. These activities and social relationships are also important to foster development of necessary lifeskills, such as forming and maintaining friendships, increasing communication skills, and handling interpersonal relationships and dating.

Historically, adult-supervised recreational activities in safe environments—which are routinely available for heterosexual youth—have not been available for LGBT youth. Instead, these youth have had to find their own social outlets, many of which are not supervised by adults. When LGBT youth are not allowed to develop in the context of normative adolescent social and institutional supports, identity is compartmentalized or "split off," increasing isolation, depression, risky behaviors, and negative health outcomes.

Caregivers and staff members should ensure that LGBT youth are aware of and have access to social and recreational services and events consistent with their interests and geared toward the community with which they identify. Conversely, staff and caregivers should not force youth to participate in activities or groups that denigrate or discriminate against LGBT youth or that simply decline to acknowledge their existence. For example, foster parents should permit a lesbian teen to attend a supervised youth support group at an LGBT community center, and they should ensure that the young woman is aware that these services are available and that she has the required transportation to participate. Likewise, foster parents should not compel the same young woman to attend religious services during which she is condemned because of her sexual orientation. Child welfare and juvenile justice agencies should maintain updated lists of local LGBT-supportive services in the area and should ensure that these resource lists are made available to all caregivers and staff members.

Agencies should also make an effort to provide parity in recreational activities for all youth, consonant with reasonable rules regarding socializing outside of the home or facility. Any limitations on a youth's social interactions should be equally applied and rationally related to the youth's safety or best interest. If heterosexual youth are encouraged and permitted to attend a high school prom, LGBT youth should be allowed to attend a local prom organized for LGBT youth. If heterosexual youth are permitted to go on overnight visits, LGBT should be allowed to do the same. If youth are allowed to participate in extracurricular school activities, the appropriate person should give LGBT youth permission to participate in Gay-Straight Alliances or related activities at school.

Agencies should also ensure that their own services and programs are LGBT inclusive. For example, if facilities or programs provide books, magazines, and movies to youth, they should include materials with positive LGBT images and role models. Independent-living programs and other lifeskills development classes should provide information that specifically addresses the needs of LGBT youth who are transitioning out of state custody, including information about legal rights, finding nonjudgmental and appropriate health care, and responding to discrimination. When social workers, probation staff, providers, or caregivers present information to youth about sexuality and development, this information should be inclusive of LGBT individuals and should not present same-sex relationships or behavior, or gender-nonconforming behavior, as inappropriate or immoral.

In secure facilities that limit contact with outside services and individuals, LGBT youth should be permitted to receive and possess LGBT-supportive books and magazines to the same extent that books and magazines are generally available to youth in the facility. Program staff in secure facilities should also permit outside groups, such as LGBT community centers or other LGBT youth organizations, to provide specific programming or counseling services that address the needs and interests of LGBT youth in the facility.

CHAPTER 5

Collecting and Managing Confidential Information

Understanding the sexual orientation or gender identity of a young person in care—like all information about the youth's unique circumstances—is important for developing and implementing the case plan. This information may be relevant to decisions about detention, diversion, reunification, health or mental health services, disposition, placement, and educational services. Information about sexual orientation and gender identity, however, is also uniquely sensitive; inappropriate disclosure can subject LGBT youth to retaliation, abuse, and psychological harm. This chapter discusses how agencies can provide a safe space for LGBT youth to come out, while protecting the confidentiality of information regarding sexual orientation or gender identity.

Providing a Safe Space for LGBT Youth to Come Out

Knowing that a young person is lesbian, gay, bisexual, or transgender can help place the youth's development, behavior, and adjustment into a social context. This information may also suggest other issues to explore, including safety, social supports, family awareness and response, and health guidance. In some cases, the intake worker will know that a young person is lesbian, gay, bisexual, or transgender at the inception of the case. The youth's sexual orientation or gender identity may be related to the reason he or she is in care, the youth or family may simply offer this information, or it may be included in case files, police reports, or other documents.

More often, however, the professionals who first come in contact with the youth do not have this information. LGBT youth are in various stages of awareness and comfort with their sexual orientation and gender identity, and they may not have resolved these issues for themselves. Even if the youth internally identifies as lesbian, gay, bisexual, or transgender, he or she may still choose not to disclose this information to agency personnel. The decision to hide one's LGBT identity is reinforced by social images and expectations, and a culture in which negative and biased (homophobic and transphobic) attitudes are still common and openly expressed. One's experience of one's gender or sexual feelings may be considered an intensely private matter. Cultural mores may also influence a young person's willingness to discuss these issues.

Intake workers and other agency staff should anticipate the understandable reticence of young people to discuss issues related to their sexual orientation or gender identity—particularly before the youth know whether they will be safe if they come out. It is generally not appropriate to simply ask a direct question about sexual orientation or gender identity as part of an initial intake or assessment. Although some professionals argue that a standard intake question would normalize these discussions, experience has shown that this approach is more often seen as offensive or intimidating—even by youth who do not identify as LGBT. In fact, the direct approach may have the unintended effect of reinforcing fear and secrecy. Case managers and intake personnel should also avoid making assumptions about a young person based on his or her physical appearance or behavior. Instead, professionals working with youth should adopt an approach that helps youth feel safe to disclose information about themselves—at their own pace and on their own terms.

Intake staff should create a relaxed and unhurried atmosphere, to the extent possible. Beginning with open-ended and noncontroversial questions helps create comfort and rapport. Offering information, in addition to requesting information, makes an interview feel more like a discussion. Explaining the purpose of the interview can help allay anxiety. The intake worker should introduce herself or himself and explain the intake process and the worker's role in the process. The interviewer should avoid mechanically asking a list of questions from an intake or assessment instrument. Instead, the worker should invite discussion of topics at appropriate intervals, paying close attention to cues that may suggest discomfort or willingness to be open.

Staff members conducting an intake or assessment should be careful to use inclusive language and to ask questions in a manner that avoids implicit assumptions about the young person's sexual orientation. For example, asking a young woman whether she has a boyfriend assumes that she is heterosexual. Moreover, if the young woman simply answers no, the questioner may have missed an opportunity to learn more about her. Instead, the worker should use neutral language, such as "Do you have a boyfriend or girlfriend?" or "Is there someone who you are particularly close to?" The young person's responses—both verbal and nonverbal—will suggest appropriate follow-up questions.

The sexual orientation or gender identity of the youth may not come up in an initial intake or assessment. It may not be relevant to the immediate crisis or initial stage of the proceedings. The youth may need more time to establish rapport and comfort disclosing this information. Many youth are too young or simply not aware of these issues at the inception of the case. Some youth enter foster care as infants or young children and become aware of these issues years later. It is important, therefore, for professional staff and caregivers in every part of child welfare and juvenile justice systems to remain sensitive, alert, and open to opportunities to discuss these issues at any point in the young person's care.

Managing Confidential Information Appropriately

Generally speaking, information regarding a youth under the jurisdiction of the juvenile court—in both the child welfare and juvenile justice systems—is confidential. Client confidentiality is protected in ethical and statutory provisions governing most professionals working in child welfare or juvenile justice agencies, including social workers, probation officers, residential providers, and counselors. Attorneys representing youth in juvenile court are also obligated to maintain client confidentiality.

The purpose of confidentiality laws is to protect the person who is the subject of the information from public disclosure of sensitive and private information, although public officials often invoke these provisions to protect the interests of public agencies and institutions. This is an important distinction because all decisions regarding the management of client information should be resolved in favor of the client's interests, rather than the interests or convenience of the agency or institution.

When a young person is in state custody, child welfare and juvenile justice agencies must treat information about his or her sexual orientation or gender identity like all other confidential client information. Agency employees should not disclose this sensitive and private information without the youth's permission. It is important for agency staff to understand that disclosing a youth's sexual orientation or gender identity without the youth's permission could subject the youth to rejection, ridicule, and even violence. Premature or nonconsensual disclosure also could interrupt or derail an LGBT youth's development and adjustment, resulting in negative health effects and loss of trust. Often the young person is in the best position to understand the possible consequences of coming out. Agency professionals should respect a young person's wishes concerning the timing and nature of any disclosure of this information.

A young person might choose to disclose information about his or her sexual orientation or gender identity. For example, a transgender youth who has been kicked out by her family may decide to disclose her gender identity to her probation officer and the court to defend against or mitigate a trespassing charge. In these circumstances, confidentiality laws do not prohibit disclosure. Again, because the laws are intended to protect the interests of the youth, he or she may waive such protection and consent to specific disclosure.

In some circumstances, limited disclosure may be legally required to protect a young person's safety. Social workers and other professionals who work with children and youth are mandated reporters under most state laws. These professionals are legally required to report suspected child abuse to child protective services. Thus, a social worker or probation officer may be required to disclose that a young person's family is abusing the youth because of his or her sexual orientation or gender identity.

Case managers should actively engage young people in discussions about these issues. When disclosure is legally required, case managers should explain who is entitled to the information and why. They should also make every effort to prepare young people and support them when negative consequences arise. When disclosure is not legally required, case managers should discuss all possible alternatives and make every effort to respect the young person's wishes. These discussions should occur as soon as possible and as needed throughout the course of the professional relationship.

To ensure that agency employees respect confidential information related to a youth's sexual orientation or gender identity, agencies should have written policies regarding the management of this information. The policies should specify the following:

- All employees working with youth should have a thorough under-standing of the circumstances under which such information must be disclosed under their jurisdiction's relevant laws.

- Unless disclosure is legally required, no employee should disclose information regarding the sexual orientation or gender identity of a youth unless that person can identify a direct benefit to the youth and has discussed the matter with the youth and obtained his or her consent.

- Case managers should carefully consider the purpose, nature, and consequences of any contemplated disclosure, and they should work with the youth to balance the potential negative consequences against the benefits of disclosure.

- When disclosure is required or appropriate, the information disclosed and the means of disclosure should be limited to that which is necessary to achieve the specific beneficial purpose. For example, the fact that a youth is transgender may be important to identify an appropriate placement. Additional details regarding the youth's medical transition, however, may be completely irrelevant to this purpose and should not be disclosed.

Agencies should take affirmative steps to ensure that all employees have a thorough understanding of applicable confidentiality laws and related agency policies and procedures. To this end, agencies should provide ongoing training and supervision to all employees, contractors, and staff regarding the maintenance and disclosure of confidential information, including sexual orientation and gender identity. Because these issues can be confusing and complex, agencies should provide a mechanism for immediate case supervision to resolve questions regarding disclosure.

CHAPTER 6

Ensuring Appropriate Homes for LGBT Youth

Youth in out-of-home care often endure frequent placement changes and multiple transitions. The lack of consistent, stable caregivers has been recognized as a major factor in impairing a young person's ability to form and maintain healthy relationships. Multiple short-term placements also deprive young people of the lifelong connections with caring adults that are crucial to their successful transition to adulthood.

LGBT youth are particularly vulnerable to "failed" placements, multiple rejections, and frequent transitions. Many systemic problems contribute to agencies' failure to provide continuity of care to LGBT youth. The most obvious problem is the chronic shortage of competent caregivers and appropriate placement options, which is, in turn, exacerbated by the failure to adequately train and support existing caregivers. Without a continuum of placement options, workers cannot make individualized decisions and often respond to problems by simply changing the placement again and again. These systemic failures affect all youth in care. They are particularly acute for LGBT youth, however, who face the additional complications caused by discriminatory attitudes and behavior at all levels of the system. For these youth, placement changes are often prompted by overt discrimination or harassment from peers, caregivers, and staff. LGBT youth may also run away from placements in which they do not feel welcome or accepted.

This chapter discusses concrete steps agencies can take to improve the quality of care provided to LGBT youth in placement, including:

- making individualized placement decisions,
- increasing and diversifying placement options available to LGBT youth, and
- supporting caregivers who are committed to caring for LGBT youth.

Making Individualized Placement Decisions

To identify appropriate homes for openly LGBT youth, gender-nonconforming youth, or youth who may be perceived as lesbian, gay, or gender variant, placement staff should work with each youth to identify homes or other settings that meet his or her individual needs. To the extent that it is developmentally appropriate, the young person should be actively involved in identifying an appropriate caregiver. Placement staff should place the LGBT youth in the most family-like setting that is appropriate and ensure that potential caregivers understand and practice inclusive, nondiscriminatory care.

In an effort to provide safe, LGBT-affirming services, several jurisdictions have developed specialized group homes for dependent and delinquent LGBT youth. These facilities can be an important resource for LGBT youth who prefer or need a more structured group setting. Placement staff should not assume, however, that every LGBT youth needs or wants to be placed in congregate care or exclusively with other LGBT youth. Many LGBT youth prefer to be with families or in a more diverse group setting.

Nor should the existence of specialized group homes circumvent agencies' obligation to place youth in the least restrictive, most family-like setting appropriate to meet each youth's individual needs. Outcomes for LGBT youth, like all youth, are significantly improved when they are placed with a family rather than in an institutional setting. Placement with a family enhances opportunities for permanence, as well as contact with siblings and other family members, and helps support the youth's successful transition to adulthood.

Agencies should also employ targeted recruitment strategies to identify potential caregivers for individual LGBT youth. Careful investigation often yields extended family members, friends of the youth or family, and other adults known to the youth who are willing to assume responsibility for the young person's custody and care. Agencies have successfully employed expanded and targeted recruitment strategies to find homes for infants with special health care needs, older youth, sibling groups, and other children who have been labeled as difficult to place or unadoptable. These same strategies can help move agencies toward a more inclusive, competent model of care, as well as ensure the availability of appropriate care for all youth in care, including LGBT youth.

Placement with families also has the same benefits for delinquent youth as it does for dependent youth. Nevertheless, many juvenile probation departments do not routinely place delinquent youth with families. Particularly for delinquent youth whose alleged offense is related to their LGBT identity or who have been rejected by their birthfamilies, placement with relatives, unrelated guardians, or foster families should be part of the continuum of placement options when secure confinement is unnecessary.

Increasing and Diversifying Placement Options

Agencies faced with a shortage of placement options cannot make individualized decisions tailored to the strengths and needs of specific youth. Too often, placement staff make decisions based on available beds rather than the young person's individual characteristics. This approach can lead to disastrous results for LGBT youth, who may be subjected to a series of insensitive or overtly discriminatory caregivers. Child welfare and juvenile justice agencies should engage in creative strategies to increase and diversify their placement resources.

Specifically, agencies should take affirmative steps to recruit caregivers, providers, and staff members who share the agency's goal of providing excellent care to all youth in the agency's custody—including LGBT youth. As part of the effort to increase LGBT-friendly resources, when recruiting foster parents, agencies should intentionally reach out to LGBT families and communities, inclusive faith communities, and community organizations whose members embrace diversity and inclusion.

Supporting Caregivers of LGBT Youth

Child welfare and juvenile justice agencies should take concrete steps to support and retain caregivers who are committed to serving LGBT youth. At the outset, agencies should provide sufficient training to all caregivers so these individuals are prepared to deliver competent care to LGBT youth. These trainings should be mandatory and ongoing and should address the following topics:

- a review of vocabulary and definitions relevant to LGBT youth;
- an exploration of myths and stereotypes regarding LGBT youth and adults;

- developmental issues and adaptive strategies for LGBT children and youth;

- positive development of LGBT adolescents;

- a review of the coming-out process and information about how family and adults can support a young person who is in the process of coming out;

- a discussion of how sexual orientation or gender identity may relate to the reasons the youth is in state custody;

- approaches to working with the families of LGBT youth and an understanding of how their acceptance or rejection affects the young person's health, mental health, and well-being;

- creating an inclusive environment for LGBT youth in child welfare and juvenile justice systems;

- implementation of the nondiscrimination and grievance policies; and

- agency and community resources available to serve LGBT youth and their families.

Agencies should use continuing education and other means of disseminating new information and pertinent research findings in the rapidly developing field of youth development, including emerging information on the needs and care of LGBT adolescents and their families. In addition to formal training, supervisors and managers should use case planning, general and clinical supervision, and regular performance evaluations as opportunities to reinforce the messages conveyed in ongoing training.

Agencies should also respond promptly and constructively to problems that arise in placements. LGBT youth who encounter discrimination, harassment, or other problems in their placements need ready access to agency personnel to initiate a problem-solving process. Likewise, caregivers and staff members need agency support to address issues related to the care of LGBT youth. Well-intentioned caregivers may need help understanding the experiences of LGBT youth, how to apply the agency's nondiscrimination policy, and options for resolving complex questions.

Agency policies should provide access to a prompt and inclusive process for resolving problems that arise in a youth's placement. The process should involve all relevant parties, including the youth; should reflect the agency's policies and values; and should emphasize mutual respect, fairness, and consensus building. The participants should avoid assuming that the youth is always the problem or that a change in placement is always the best solution. Many agencies convene a meeting whenever any placement decision or change is contemplated. In addition to the youth, the participants might include the caregiver, family members, teacher, social worker, probation officer, and any other person who might contribute to identifying a solution. The goal of these sessions is to collectively identify a solution that promotes continuity of care and mutual respect and understanding. Agencies should ensure that the focus of these meetings is on the youth's needs and that the youth is empowered to take the lead in identifying potential solutions.

CHAPTER 7

LGBT Youth in Institutional Settings

The law, as well as sound practice, generally supports the use of the least restrictive and most family-like placement possible for each individual youth. In some circumstances, however, placement in group care may be appropriate or necessary to meet the needs of individual LGBT youth or otherwise achieve the goals identified in the case plan or disposition. Group facilities range from unlocked facilities such as group homes, shelters, camps, and ranches, to more restrictive institutions such as treatment facilities, detention facilities, correctional facilities, and psychiatric hospitals. These facilities may house from a few to hundreds of youth at any given time. The nature of their programs, including the structure, level of restrictiveness, and average length of stay, varies according to the facility's purpose.

Although the size, purpose, and character of congregate care facilities vary tremendously, group care, in general, presents potential risks to the safety and well-being of LGBT youth. Child welfare and juvenile justice agencies have a legal obligation to protect the safety of LGBT youth housed in group care (*Alexander S. v. Boyd,* 1998; *Hernandez ex rel, Hernandez v. Texas Department of Protective and Regulatory Services,* 2004; *R.G. v. Koller,* 2006). This chapter discusses concrete policies and practices to meet these constitutional requirements.

Housing and Classification of LGBT Youth

In most congregate care facilities, intake staff conduct an assessment or initial screening to determine where and with whom the youth will be housed in the facility. This process may be more formal in larger facilities, in which there are a range of housing options. In secure detention or correctional facilities, this process is referred to as "classification."

Before placing LGBT youth in an institutional setting, placement staff should carefully investigate the facility's policies and practices regarding housing and classifying LGBT residents. Many institutions have formal or informal policies governing the classification or housing of lesbian or gay youth—often without regard to the individual characteristics of the youth. Often, these policies are based on myths or stereotypes about sexual orientation or gender identity. Agencies should ensure that all group care facilities make appropriate, individualized classification and housing decisions.

Facilities should not automatically classify youth who are known or perceived to be LGBT as sex offenders, unless the youth actually has a history of committing sexual offenses. This practice places LGBT youth who are already more vulnerable to harassment or violence with youth identified as predators, creating a very high risk of injury.

Facilities should not automatically isolate or segregate lesbian or gay youth "for their protection." Even when motivated by good intentions, this practice is unconstitutional and has the effect of punishing vulnerable youth (*R.G. v. Koller*, 2006). Segregation also deprives LGBT young people of education, programming, and recreational opportunities, as well as contact with their peers, thereby increasing their boredom, despair, and loneliness.

Facilities should not prohibit lesbian or gay youth from having roommates. This practice is often based on the misconception that lesbian and gay youth are more likely to engage in sexual activity than their heterosexual peers—regardless of the sexual orientation of their roommate. These punitive measures further stigmatize and isolate vulnerable youth, and completely fail to address the underlying ignorance and fear that creates the threat to their safety and well-being.

Rather than relying on rigid classification rules, intake staff should work with individual LGBT youth to identify the most appropriate housing assignment in a group care facility, given the youth's specific preferences, needs, and characteristics. Staff should make assignments to a unit, room, or roommate according to the youth's preferences, personality, background, age, developmental status, health status, sophistication, social skills, behavioral history, and other factors that might influence his or her adjustment and contribute to a safe and successful experience. If a young person feels more secure in a single-occupancy room and this option is available, the staff should take his or her preference into consideration. Similarly, if the youth prefers having a roommate, staff should try to accommodate the request, if possible. Staff should never, however, place an LGBT youth in a room with another youth who is overtly hostile toward or demeaning of LGBT individuals.

Protecting the Safety and Well-Being of Transgender Youth

In almost all group care facilities, a youth's gender is a crucial factor in deciding where to house him or her, and with whom. Most facilities classify youth according to their anatomical sex, which is generally consistent with their gender identity. For transgender youth—whose gender identity is different from their anatomical sex—however, these policies are insensitive and can cause unnecessary humiliation, harassment, psychological trauma, and even violence.

Intake staff should not assign transgender youth to the boys or girls unit strictly according to their anatomical sex. Rather, staff should accept the gender identity of the youth in question, even if that means forgoing the general methods used to define youth as male or female for the purposes of classification. Staff should make individualized classification and housing decisions based on the emotional and physical well-being of the specific transgender youth, and they should consider the youth's evaluation of his or her safety, the availability of privacy, the range of housing options available, and any recommendations from the youth's mental health providers regarding appropriate housing or classification for him or her.

Many facilities have successfully accommodated transgender youth by working closely with the young person, demonstrating a willingness to be flexible, and staying focused on the unique characteristics of that particular youth. In most cases, it will be appropriate to house transgender youth according to their current gender identity, not their anatomical sex, although it may be important to provide them with additional privacy for showering or a single room for sleeping. Some facilities place transgender youth in mixed-gender units or programs, which reduces their vulnerability to violence and harassment and eliminates the difficulties associated with finding a gender-appropriate unit. Some facilities have gone even farther—using the experience of serving transgender youth as an opportunity to examine the justifications for strict gender segregation and creating opportunities for coeducational programming and housing.

In many facilities, bathroom and shower accommodations offer little or no privacy. Often, facilities require the youth housed in a particular unit to shower and use the toilet in each others' presence, under the supervision of a staff member of the same sex as the youth. For transgender youth who are housed in units according to their anatomical sex, this situation poses serious risks to their safety and well-being.

To avoid subjecting a transgender youth to unnecessary risk of harm, the staff should work with the youth to determine the best solution for using bathroom and shower facilities. Appropriate solutions might include:

- Installing privacy doors or other barriers on bathroom stalls and showers that also permit reasonable staff supervision.

- Making single-use bathroom and shower facilities available to transgender youth.

- Permitting transgender youth to use the bathroom and shower facilities before or after the other youth on the unit.

Facilities should make similar accommodations to ensure that transgender youth have sufficient privacy when dressing and undressing.

Programmatic Protections

LGBT youth placed in congregate settings are substantially more likely to be subjected to hostility, harassment, violence, and sexual assault than their non-LGBT counterparts. Name calling, ridicule, and overt hostility are ubiquitous and often an accepted part of the institutional culture. Left unchecked, these behaviors and attitudes can escalate and lead to even more serious and harmful harassment and violence. Child welfare and juvenile justice professionals should be aware of these dangers and should adopt policies and practices that protect the safety of all youth, including LGBT youth.

To meet this obligation, agencies should:

- develop and implement a nondiscrimination policy and ensure that all youth and staff are aware of the policy;

- provide initial and ongoing staff training on strategies for maintaining a safe, humane environment and responding to harassment and discrimination toward LGBT youth;

- use small facilities with multiple housing options and a range of support services to meet the needs of individual youth;

- use group care for the shortest period necessary; and

- transition youth as soon as possible to less restrictive settings.

Agencies should also ensure sufficient numbers of staff to closely supervise youth and maximize the opportunities for interaction between staff and residents. Supervision of smaller groups of youth enables staff to develop relationships with residents and prevents the need for more intrusive or depersonalized surveillance. Incidents of harassment or violence toward LGBT youth are much less likely to occur or to escape the staff's attention when a facility has high staff-to-resident ratios. Facilities should also provide high-quality programming that keeps youth out of their rooms and engages them in meaningful activities.

Group care staff should consistently model and communicate the message that every person is entitled to respect and dignity and that disrespect or intolerance of any kind is not permitted. Staff should promptly intervene whenever a young person uses a homophobic or transphobic epithet or engages in behavior that is discriminatory or demeaning toward LGBT individuals or groups. Depending on the nature of the incident, it may be most appropriate to treat it as an opportunity to discuss the issue of homophobia or transphobia generally or the facility's policy of treating everyone respectfully. If a young person engages in serious or repeated incidents of harassment or violence toward LGBT youth, however, staff should not hesitate to impose meaningful consequences, such as separation of that youth from the group or transfer to a more restrictive setting, if appropriate. Similarly, agency personnel should take prompt disciplinary action against any staff member who engages in disrespectful or discriminatory behavior toward LGBT youth.

CHAPTER 8

Providing Appropriate Health, Mental Health, and Education Services to LGBT Youth

When the state assumes custody of a young person, it is obligated to ensure his or her overall well-being (see, e.g., *K.H. v. Morgan,* 1990, explaining that the Constitution requires state officials to take steps to prevent children in state institutions from deteriorating physically and psychologically). To this end, child welfare and juvenile justice agencies must protect the safety of LGBT youth in their care and ensure that these youth receive appropriate medical, mental health, and educational services responsive to their individual needs. Sometimes, agency personnel deliver these services onsite. More often, however, other public agencies, such as the health department or the school district, or private providers with whom child welfare and juvenile justice agencies contract, provide these services. Regardless of the setting in which these services are delivered, however, agencies maintain the obligation to ensure that health and mental health providers, as well as educators, are capable of ensuring the safety of LGBT youth and providing appropriate care and services.

In this chapter, the authors elaborate on the responsibility of child welfare and juvenile justice agencies to ensure that the LGBT youth in their care and custody receive health, mental health, and educational services that are appropriate, nondiscriminatory, and consistent with applicable professional standards.

Providing Inclusive, Nondiscriminatory Health Care to LGBT Youth

Youth who enter out-of-home care are at greater risk of having serious health problems due to inadequate access to health care and lack of connection with an adult who attends to and monitors their health care on a consistent basis. LGBT adolescents experience the same range of health and mental health challenges as youth in out-of-home care and other adolescents in general, but their vulnerability is increased by the effect of social stigma and the lack of accurate information and provider training about their needs. Stigma has social, behavioral, and health-related consequences that can increase high-risk behaviors, such as unprotected sex and substance abuse, and intensify psychological distress and risk for suicide (Ryan & Futterman, 1997). In addition, LGBT youth are at high risk for victimization in school, community, and institutional settings and among rejecting families. Victimization has a range of negative outcomes, including mental health problems and post-traumatic stress.

LGBT youth often are afraid to disclose their sexual orientation or gender identity to health care providers. Unfortunately, many health care providers have negative attitudes toward LGBT patients and clients, and a range of studies have reported provider bias and discriminatory care (Ryan & Futterman, 1997). When gay or lesbian youth disclose their sexual orientation, some providers minimize or deny their concerns on the grounds that same-gender sexual behavior is simply a phase that adolescents will grow out of. Other providers are simply ignorant of the experiences and health concerns that affect LGBT youth and do not recognize the relevance of sexual orientation or gender identity to the youth's health status.

Even providers who are not uncomfortable with or biased in caring for LGBT individuals may miss the opportunity to identify and address the specific health concerns of LGBT youth. Trained in a heterosexual model, providers may use terminology or questions that assume that the young person is heterosexual. For example, providers often inquire indirectly about the sexual activity of girls by asking if they would like to discuss birth control. Providers may also assume that a youth who identifies as gay has only male sexual partners. This may or may not be the case. Whether they identify as LGBT or heterosexual, adolescents may experiment with various sexual practices as they mature.

Child welfare and juvenile justice agencies should ensure that trained providers offer competent, sensitive health assessments and treatment to LGBT youth. The Family Acceptance Project is developing risk-resiliency assessment materials for multidisciplinary providers to quickly assess risk and resilience for LGBT youth and to identify family dynamics for education and intervention. In particular, agencies should ensure that all LGBT youth entering state care receive a comprehensive health assessment from a non-judgmental provider as soon as possible (see Ryan & Futterman, 1997, for basic guidelines for mental health assessment, primary care, and HIV-related care). The assessment should include an interview to identify possible risks, health guidance information, and a routine physical examination. The interview with the young person should be inclusive of LGBT issues, and the interviewer should be careful to avoid assumptions about the youth's sexual orientation or gender identity and should use inclusive language.

Child welfare and juvenile justice agencies should also ensure that LGBT youth in their care receive comprehensive sexuality education that is inclusive and affirming of LGBT people. The sexual education curriculum should include the areas of sexually transmitted disease, pregnancy prevention, and safe sex practices that are inclusive of LGBT youth.

Providing Inclusive, Nondiscriminatory Mental Health Care to LGBT Youth

LGBT youth commonly experience chronic stress related to harassment, the need for vigilance to protect against discrimination and abuse, coming out to family and friends, and having one's sexual orientation discovered (Ryan & Futterman, 1997). Chronic stress can lead to increased levels of depression and anxiety. Several studies, including population-based studies, indicate a higher risk of suicide ideation and attempts among lesbian, gay, and bisexual youth, compared with their heterosexual peers (see, for example, Garofalo, Wolf, Kessel, Palfrey, & DuRant, 1998). LGBT youth are also at risk for inappropriate mental health treatment, including misdiagnosis of gender identity disorder, involuntary institutionalization, and reparative therapy or other interventions designed to change their sexual orientation or gender identity. During the past several years, reparative therapy has been increasingly promoted by conservative groups, although the major professional associations caution against its use to try to change an individual's sexual orientation (see American Academy of Pediatrics, 1993; American Psychiatric Association, 1998).[11] Child welfare

---

[11] In 1993, the American Academy of Pediatrics (1993) issued a Policy Statement on Homosexuality and Adolescence stating that "therapy directed specifically at changing sexual orientation is contraindicated, since it can provoke guilt and anxiety while having little or no potential for achieving changes in orientation" (p. 633). In 1998, the American Psychiatric Association released a policy statement asserting that it "opposes any psychiatric treatment, such as 'reparative' or 'conversion' therapy which is based upon the assumption that homosexuality per se is a mental disorder or based upon a prior assumption that the patient should change his/her homosexual orientation" (p. 1), and in 2000, the association determined that "'reparative' therapists have not produced any rigorous scientific research to substantiate their claims of cure" (p. 1). Also in 1997, the American Psychological Association (APA) issued the *Resolution on Appropriate Therapeutic Responses to Sexual Orientation*, stating, "The APA opposes portrayals of lesbian, gay, bisexual youth and adults as mentally ill due to their sexual orientation and supports the dissemination of accurate information about sexual orientation, and mental health, and appropriate interventions in order to counter bias that is based in ignorance or unfounded beliefs about sexual orientation."

and juvenile justice agencies should not employ or contract with mental health providers who engage in reparative therapy or other interventions designed to change a young person's sexual orientation or gender identity.

Mental health providers working with LGBT youth should be prepared to address disclosure and integration of sexual orientation or gender identity, sexual behavior and risk reduction, use of alcohol and drugs to manage low self-esteem, the effects of discrimination, and the availability of support systems, including families, in and outside the LGBT community (Ryan & Futterman, 1997). Providers should provide nonjudgmental counseling and support and should affirm the young person's intrinsic worth regardless of his or her sexual orientation or gender identity. When a young person is unsure or confused about these issues, the provider should support the youth's integral development and should not attempt to steer the youth in a direction that affirms the provider's choice or bias.

Similarly, neither agency personnel nor the mental health providers with whom they contract should require LGBT youth to participate in sex-offender treatment or counseling based solely on the youths' sexual orientation or gender identity. These interventions are designed to address pathological sexual behavior and are only appropriate for youth who have a history of sexually assaultive conduct. If an LGBT youth has a sex offense adjudication and is receiving sex-offender treatment, agencies should ensure that this treatment is nondiscriminatory and does not criminalize or pathologize the youth's LGBT identity.

Providing Transgender Youth with Appropriate Health and Mental Health Care

Transgender youth may present health concerns distinct from those common to lesbian, gay, or bisexual youth generally. Transgender youth experience very high levels of stigmatization, which may increase their feelings of depression and hopelessness. They may also experience significant distress because their body does not correspond to their gender identity. Some transgender youth may be at high risk for HIV transmission, infection, and related health problems after obtaining hormones from the streets and using them without medical supervision. To address these concerns, transgender youth need access to experienced, appropriately trained, and affirming health and mental health providers.

The incongruity between a transgender youth's gender identity and anatomical sex can cause intense feelings of conflict and emotional pain (Israel & Tarver, 1997). The medical term for this condition is "gender identity disorder," which is also known as "transsexualism" or "gender dysphoria" (American Psychiatric Association, *Diagnostic and Statistical Manual of Mental Disorders*, 4th ed., text rev. [*DSM-IV-TR*], 2000a). Gender identity disorder has two components, both of which must be present for an individual diagnosis. First, a person must have a strong and persistent cross-gender identification, that is, a strong and persistent desire to be, or the insistence that he or she is, of the other sex (*DSM-IV-TR*, 2000a, pp. 532–533). Second, one must have persistent discomfort about one's anatomical sex or a sense of inappropriateness in the gender role corresponding to one's anatomical sex, which in turn causes "clinically significant distress or impairment in social, occupational, or other important areas of functioning" (*DSM-IV-TR*, 2000a, pp. 532–533).

Proper treatment for gender identity disorder includes counseling and medical care that helps the individual bring his or her physical body more in line with his or her internal self-identification (Meyer et al., 2001). Current medical standards seek to respect the dignity and autonomy of individuals with gender identity disorder by requiring health care professionals to acknowledge an individual's self-designated gender identification (Beemer, 1996; Israel & Tarver, 1997; Meyer et al., 2001).

In the past, some practitioners tried to "cure" individuals with gender identity disorder through aversion therapies and other techniques intended to alter cross-gender identification (Gelder & Marks, 1969). These efforts were not only unsuccessful, but caused severe psychological and, in some cases, even physical damage (Mallon, 1999c). Today, efforts to alter a person's core gender identity are viewed as both futile and unethical (Israel & Tarver, 1997; Mallon, 1999c). Accordingly, the treatment paradigm has shifted from attempting to cure an individual with gender identity disorder "to facilitating acceptance and management of a gender role transition" (Bockting & Coleman, 1992; Meyer et al., 2001).

Many transgender people engage in medical care that helps externalize their internal gender identity by masculinizing or feminizing their appearance. This medical care may include taking hormones to help them develop secondary sex characteristics consistent with their gender identity. For many transgender people, hormone treatment leads to improved mental and emotional stability, enhanced success in employment and education, and reduction of self-destructive behaviors such as substance abuse or even suicide (Green & Flemming, 1990; Pfäfflin & Junge, 1992/1998). The Harry Benjamin International Gender Dysphoria Association (HBIGDA)[12] has developed internationally recognized professional medical standards for the diagnosis and treatment of gender identity disorders in both youth and adults (Meyer et al., 2001). The HBIGDA standards of care provide a general protocol for the provision of transgender health care, guiding providers on how to determine when cross-gender hormone treatment and gender-confirming surgeries are medically necessary for treating gender identity disorder (Meyer et al., 2001).

Providing access to medical and mental health professionals who can help assess whether hormone treatment is appropriate for transgender and gender-nonconforming youth is essential in providing appropriate care for these youth. When youth have no access to professionals who can help them determine their needs for such care, they often turn to street economies to buy hormones. Taking hormones without medical supervision can result in serious medical complications. In addition, many youth who turn to the street to find these supplements may engage in dangerous or illegal activity, such as prostitution or theft, to pay for them.

To appropriately address the health care needs of transgender youth, agencies should:

- use health and mental health providers who are knowledgeable about the health needs of transgender youth and who understand gender identity disorder and the professional standards of care for transgender people,

- permit transgender youth to continue to receive all transition-related treatment they started prior to involvement with the child welfare or juvenile justice agencies, and

- provide any necessary authorization for transition-related treatments when they are medically necessary according to accepted professional standards.

---

[12] Harry Benjamin International Gender Dysphoria Association is a professional organization devoted to the understanding and treatment of gender identity disorders. The organization's membership includes approximately 350 licensed professionals in the disciplines of medicine, including internal medicine, endocrinology, plastic and reconstructive surgery, urology, gynecology, psychiatry, nursing, psychology, and neuropsychology, from 20 countries, including the United States. See www.hbigda.org.

Ensuring Safe and Nondiscriminatory Educational Opportunities for LGBT Youth

Generally, youth in out-of-home care face disruptions in their education, which puts them at greater risk for lower school performance. This risk is heightened for LGBT youth or those who are perceived to be lesbian, gay, bisexual, or transgender due to pervasive harassment and discrimination in school settings. The widespread extent of anti-gay discrimination and harassment in schools, as well as the dangerous consequences, have been well-documented (see, for example, California Safe Schools Coalition, 2004; Human Rights Watch, 2001).

Population-based studies of youth in schools show significantly higher rates of victimization among lesbian, gay, and bisexual youth compared with their heterosexual peers. In the Massachusetts Youth Risk Behavior Study, lesbian, gay, and bisexual youth were more than four times as likely to have been threatened with a weapon at school, more than three times as likely to have been in a fight that required medical attention, and nearly five times as likely as heterosexual youth to have missed school because they were afraid (Garafalo et al., 1998). Compared with their heterosexual peers, lesbian, gay, and bisexual youth were also more than three times as likely to have attempted suicide during the past 12 months.

Among students in the California adolescent risk behavior survey, 7.5% of middle and high school students (200,000 students) reported being bullied or harassed because they were known or perceived to be gay (California Safe Schools Coalition, 2004). Students who were victimized were more than three times as likely to seriously consider suicide, develop a suicide plan (a signal of serious intent), or miss school because they felt unsafe.

Recent research has shown that anti-gay victimization has long-term adverse effects that persist into adulthood and affect health and mental health and well-being. In the Family Acceptance Project, Ryan and Diaz (2005) found that LGBT young adults who had experienced high levels of anti-gay victimization in middle or high school were more than twice as likely to report symptoms of depression and substance abuse problems, three times as likely to report suicide attempts, and more than twice as likely to have put themselves at risk for HIV infection during the past six months, compared with their LGBT peers who reported low levels of anti-gay victimization during adolescence. Young adults who reported high levels of anti-gay victimization in school had significantly lower levels of self-esteem, social support, and life satisfaction than their LGBT peers who reported low levels of victimization, which shows the corrosive effect of victimization on all aspects of a young person's life.

Child welfare and juvenile justice agencies are obligated to ensure that youth in their custody receive appropriate educational services. To ensure the safety of LGBT youth and to maximize the continuity and success of the educational services they receive, agencies should scrutinize and closely monitor offsite and onsite educational programs. The Family Acceptance Project is developing guidelines for child welfare agencies and caregivers for preventing and managing school victimization of LGBT children and adolescents.[13] Agency personnel must take seriously any report of harassment or violence in educational settings and hold schools accountable for appropriate protections for LGBT students.

If agency personnel learn that an LGBT youth in their care is experiencing harassment or discrimination in school, an agency representative should take prompt action to address these behaviors and ensure that the youth is safe and treated fairly. Agencies should include the youth when determining how to address the situation. Some appropriate actions include:

- notifying school officials of the harassment or discrimination and following up to make sure that they take appropriate remedial steps to respond to the harassment and discrimination,

- meeting with the youth's teacher, and

- contacting the police if the youth has been injured or is in fear for his or her safety.

If the harassment and discrimination continues, agency personnel or caregivers should work with the youth to determine the best course of action. Examples may include:

- bringing the harassment to the attention of the school board;

- filing an official complaint with the appropriate state agency;

- consulting with an attorney about possible legal remedies; and

- transferring the youth to another school, although agency personnel should only use this option if no other solutions exist.

---

13 Available in fall 2006.

In addition to the harassment and discrimination that LGBT youth experience in educational settings, transgender youth often face unique barriers preventing their safe access to school. School officials may refuse to allow transgender students to wear clothing that corresponds with their gender identity or refuse to recognize a student's chosen name and pronoun. Schools often fail to provide transgender students with access to safe bathrooms or locker rooms, and they may prohibit transgender youth from fully participating in extracurricular activities that are gender segregated.

Child welfare and juvenile justice agencies should be prepared to advocate in the schools on behalf of transgender youth in their care to address these problems. Before a transgender youth starts at a new school, it may be appropriate for agency staff to meet with school officials to inquire about the school's experiences working with transgender youth and to establish expectations.

Glossary

Anatomical sex An individual's sex, male or female, based on the appearance of their sexual organs.

Biological sex An individual's sex, male or female, based on their sex chromosomes.

Birth sex The sex, male or female, that is noted on an individual's birth certificate.

Classification The process by which intake staff at a congregate care facility assess where and with whom youth will be housed.

Coming out The process of self-identifying as lesbian, gay, bisexual, or transgender (LGBT) or disclosing one's LGBT identity to others.

Congregate care Out-of-home settings in which youth are housed in groups and supervised by staff members who do not live with the youth. These settings are more institutional, restrictive, and impersonal than family settings.

Family-centered care Viewing youth in care as members of families and communities, rather than just as individuals.

Fictive kin Individuals unrelated to youth in care through either birth or adoptive families, but whom the youth views as kin. Caseworkers are encouraged to ask youth about fictive kin and to allow them to take part in permanency planning for the youth.

Gender identity A person's internal identification or self-image as male or female, which is usually established by age 3.

Gender identity disorder A strong, persistent desire to be the opposite sex, as well as a persistent discomfort about one's anatomical sex or a sense of inappropriateness in the gender role corresponding to one's anatomical sex.

Gender nonconforming Individuals whose behaviors, characteristics, mannerisms, or dress are perceived by others as inappropriate for their anatomical sex based on cultural beliefs or stereotypes.

Gender roles Social and cultural beliefs about appropriate male or female behavior, which children usually internalize between ages 3 and 7.

Legal permanence A permanent family, whether through adoption or guardianship, for a youth in care.

LGBT Lesbian, gay, bisexual, and transgender.

Mandated reporter Someone, such as a teacher, who is legally required to report suspected child abuse to the local child protection agency.

Nondiscrimination policy A written policy that explicitly includes sexual orientation and gender identity and that prohibits anti-LGBT harassment and discrimination.

Permanence A permanent connection with at least one committed adult who provides a safe, stable home for a youth exiting care.

Physical permanence A permanent place to live.

Relational permanence A permanent relationship with an adult.

Reparative therapy An intervention intended to change an individual's sexual orientation from homosexual to heterosexual, which is not condoned by the American Academy of Pediatrics, the American Psychiatric Association, and other major professional associations. Agencies should not permit or condone staff, caregivers, community providers, or contractors to use these interventions.

Self-identification One's own identification of one's gender identity or sexual orientation. Increasingly, LGBT youth are self-identifying during adolescence.

Sex offender Someone who commits a sex-based crime. LGBT youth are sometimes wrongly viewed as sex offenders by foster parents and congregate care staff. This is unconstitutional and dangerous for the youth.

Sex roles See **gender roles.**

Sexual orientation An enduring emotional, romantic, sexual, and affectional attraction to others that is shaped at an early age. It varies from exclusively homosexual, to bisexual, to exclusively heterosexual.

Throwaway youth Youth whose parents have ejected them from the family home.

Transgender person A person whose gender identity (their understanding of themselves as male or female) does not correspond with their anatomical sex. A transgender woman is a woman whose birth sex was male but who understands herself to be female. A transgender man is a man whose birth sex was female but who understands himself to be male.

Transphobia Fear of or enmity toward transgender or gender-nonconforming people, which may result in prejudice or discrimination.

References

Alexander S. v. Boyd, 876 F. Supp. 773 (D.S.C. 1995), aff'd in part and rev'd in part on other grounds, 113 F.3d 1373 (4th Cir. 1997), cert. denied, 118 S.Ct. 880 (1998).

American Academy of Pediatrics. (1993). Homosexuality and adolescence. *Pediatrics, 92,* 631–634.

American Psychiatric Association. (1997). *Homosexual and bisexual issues.* Washington, DC: Author.

American Psychiatric Association. (1998). *Position statement on psychiatric treatment and sexual orientation.* Washington, DC: Author. Available from http://www.psych.org/edu/other_res/lib_archives/archives/199820.pdf.

American Psychiatric Association. (2000a). *Diagnostic and statistical manual of mental disorders* (4th ed., text rev.). Washington, DC: American Psychiatric Association.

American Psychiatric Association. (2000b). *Position statement on therapies focused on attempts to change sexual orientation (reparative or conversion therapies).* Washington, DC: Author. Available from http://www.psych.org/edu/other_res/lib_archives/archives/200001.pdf.

American Psychological Association. (1997). *Resolution on appropriate therapeutic responses to sexual orientation.* Washington, DC: Author. Available from http://www.apa.org/pi/sexual.html.

American Psychological Association. (n.d.). *Answers to your questions about sexual orientation and homosexuality.* Washington, DC: Author.

Beemer, B. R. (1996). Gender dysphoria update. *Journal of Psychosocial Nursing and Mental Health Services, 34*(4), 12–19.

Benard, B. (2004). *Resiliency: What we have learned.* San Francisco: WestEd.

Berberet, H. (2004, July). *Living in the shadows: An assessment of housing needs among San Diego's LGBTQ youth in living outside the home.* Paper presented at the American Psychological Association annual meeting, Honolulu, HI.

Bockting, W. O., & Coleman, E. (1992). A comprehensive approach to the treatment of gender dysphoria. *Journal of Psychology & Human Sexuality, 5*(4), 131.

California Safe Schools Coalition. (2004). *A safe place to learn: Consequences of harassment based on actual or perceived sexual orientation or gender non-conformity and steps for making schools safer.* San Francisco: Author.

Child Welfare League of America & Lambda Legal. (2006). *Out of the margins: A report on regional listening forums highlighting the experiences of lesbian, gay, bisexual, transgender, and questioning youth in care.* Washington, DC: Author.

Cochran, B. N., Stewart, A. J., Joshua, B. A., Ginzler, A., & Cauce, A. M. (2002). Challenges faced by homeless sexual minorities: Comparison of gay, lesbian, bisexual, and transgender homeless adolescents with their heterosexual counterparts. *American Journal of Public Health, 92,* 773–777.

Cole, C. M., Emory, L. E., Huang, T., & Meyer, W. J. (1994). Treatment of gender dysphoria. *Texas Medicine, 90,* 68–72.

D'Augelli, A. R., Hershberger, S. L., & Pilkington, N. W. (1998). Lesbian, gay, and bisexual youth and their families: Disclosure of sexual orientation and its consequences. *American Journal of Orthopsychiatry, 68,* 361–371.

D'Augelli, A. R., Pilkington, N. W., & Hershberger, S. L. (2002). Incidence and mental health impact of sexual orientation victimization of lesbian, gay, and bisexual youths in school. *School Psychology Quarterly, 17,* 148–167.

DeCrescenzo, T., & Mallon, G. P. (2000). *Serving transgender youth: The role of child welfare systems.* Washington, DC: Child Welfare League of America.

Doe v. Bell, 754 N.Y.S.2d 846 (N.Y. Sup. Ct., 2003).

Freundlich, M., & Avery, R. (2005). Planning for permanency for youth in congregate care. *Child and Youth Services Review, 27,* 115–134.

Garafalo, R., Wolf, C., Kessel, S., Palfrey, J., & DuRant, R. H. (1998). The association between risk behaviors and sexual orientation among a school-based sample of adolescents. *Pediatrics, 101,* 895–902.

Gelder, M. G., & Marks, I. M. (1969). Aversion treatment in transvestism and transsexualism. In R. Green & J. Money (Eds.), *Transsexualism and sex reassignment*. Baltimore: Johns Hopkins University Press.

Green, R., & Flemming, D. (1990). Transsexual surgery follow-up: Status in the 1990's. *Annual Review of Sex Research, 1,* 163–174.

Hair, E. C., Jager, J., & Garrett, S. B. (2002). Helping teens develop healthy social skills and relationships: What the research shows about navigating adolescence. *Child Trends Research Brief.* Washington, DC: Child Trends.

Hernandez ex rel, Hernandez v. Texas Department of Protective and Regulatory Services, 380 F 3d 872, 880 (5th Cir., 2004).

Human Rights Watch. (2001). *Hatred in the hallways: Violence and discrimination against lesbian, gay, bisexual and transgender students in US schools*. New York: Author.

Israel, G. E., & Tarver, D. E. I., II. (1997). *Transgender care: Recommended guidelines, practical information, and personal accounts*. Philadelphia: Temple University Press.

Jacobs, J., & Freundlich, M. (2006). *Achieving permanency for LGBTQ youth*. Washington, DC: Child Welfare League of America.

Joint Task Force of New York City's Child Welfare Administration and the Council of Family and Child Caring Agencies. (1994). *Improving services for gay and lesbian youth in NYC's child welfare system: A task force report*. New York: Child Welfare Administration and Council of Family and Child Caring Agencies.

Kessler, S. J., & McKenna, W. (1978). *Gender: An ethnomethodological approach*. New York: John Wiley & Sons.

K.H. v. Morgan, 914 F. 2d 846, 851 (7th Cir., 1990).

Kosciw, J., & Cullen, M. K. (2001). *The school-related experiences of our nation's lesbian, gay, bisexual and transgender youth*. New York: GLSEN.

Louisell, M. (2004). *Model programs for youth permanency*. Oakland, CA: California Permanency for Youth Project.

Mallon, G. (1992). Gay and no place to go: Assessing the needs of gay and lesbian adolescents in out-of-home care settings. *Child Welfare, 71,* 547–556.

Mallon, G. P. (1994). The experience of gay and lesbian adolescents in New York City's child welfare system. In A. Siskind & F. Kunreuther (Eds.), *Report and recommendations of a joint task force of New York City's Child Welfare Administration and the Council of Family and Child Caring Agencies.* New York: Child Welfare Administration and Council of Family and Child Caring Agencies.

Mallon, G. P. (1997). Basic premises, guiding principles, and competent practices for a positive youth development approach to working with gay, lesbian, and bisexual youth in out-of-home care. *Child Welfare, 76,* 591–609.

Mallon, G. P. (1998). *We don't exactly get the welcome wagon: The experience of gay and lesbian adolescents in North America's child welfare system.* New York: Columbia University Press.

Mallon, G. P. (1999a). Gay and lesbian adolescents and their families. *Journal of Gay & Lesbian Social Services, 10*(2), 69–88.

Mallon, G. P. (1999b). *Let's get this straight: A gay- and lesbian-affirming approach to child welfare.* New York. Columbia University Press.

Mallon, G. (1999c). Practice with transgendered children. In G. Mallon (Ed.), *Social services with transgendered youth* (pp. 49, 55–58). Binghamton, NY: Haworth Press.

Mallon, G. P. (Ed.). (1999d). *Social services with transgendered youth.* New York: Haworth Press.

Mallon, G. P., Aledort, N., & Ferrera, M. (2002). There's no place like home: Achieving safety, permanency, and well-being for lesbian and gay adolescents in out-of-home care settings. *Child Welfare, 81,* 407–439.

Meyer, W. J., III, Bockting, W. O., Cohen-Kettenis, P. T., Coleman, E., Di Ceglie, D., Devor, H., et al. (2001, February). *The Harry Benjamin International Gender Dysphoria Association's standards of care for gender identity disorders* (6th ed.). Minneapolis, MN: Harry Benjamin International Gender Dysphoria Association. Retrieved April 10, 2006, from http://www.hbigda.org/Documents2/socv6.pdf.

Money, J. (1973). Gender role, gender identity, core gender identity: Usage and definition of terms. *Journal of the American Academy of Psychoanalysis, 1,* 397–403.

Neal v. Shimoda, 131 F.3d 818 (9th Cir., 1997).

North American Council on Adoptable Children. (2005). *A family for every child: Strategies to achieve permanence for older foster children and youth.* Baltimore: Annie E. Casey Foundation.

Pfäfflin, F., & Junge, A. (1998). *Sex reassignment—Thirty years of international follow-up studies; SRS: A comprehensive review, 1961–1991* (R. B. Jacobson & A. B. Meier, Trans.). Düsseldorf , Germany: Symposium. (Original work published 1992)

Reis, B., & Saewyc, E. (1999). *Eighty-three thousand youth: Selected findings of eight population-based studies as they pertain to anti-gay harassment and the safety and well-being of sexual minority students.* Seattle: Safe Schools Coalition of Washington.

R.G. v. Koller, — F. Supp.2d —, WL 291637 (D. Hawaii, 2006).

Ryan, C., & Diaz, R. (2005, February). *Family responses as a source of risk & resiliency for LGBT youth.* Paper presented at the Child Welfare League of America Preconference Institute, Washington, DC.

Ryan, C., & Futterman, D. (1997). Lesbian and gay youth: Care and counseling. *Adolescent Medicine: State of the Art Reviews, 8,* 207–374.

Ryan, C., & Futterman, D. (2001). Lesbian and gay adolescents: Identity development. *Prevention Researcher, 8*(1), 1–5.

Sanchez, R. M. (2004). *Youth perspectives on permanency.* Oakland, CA: California Permanency for Youth Project.

State v. Limon, 280 Kan. 175, 22 P.3d 122 (2005).

Troiden, R. (1988). Homosexual identity development. *Journal of Adolescent Health Care, 9,* 105–113.

U.S. Department of Health and Human Services. (2003). *National Survey of Child and Adolescent Well-Being (NSCAW).* Available from http://www.acf. dhhs.gov/programs/opre/abuse_neglect/nscaw/exesum_nscaw/exe-sum_nscaw.html.

Wald, M., & Martinez, T. (2003). *Connected by 25: Improving the life chances of the country's most vulnerable youth*. Retrieved April 7, 2006, from http://www.hewlett.org/Archives/Publications/connectedBy25.htm.

Weithorn, L. (2005). Envisioning second-order change in America's responses to troubled and troublesome youth. *Hofstra Law Review, 33*, 1305.

Model Standards Project Staff

Legal Services for Children

Allyson Bogie, Administrative Assistant

Vandnez Lam, MSW, Social Worker

Kayniee Lopez, MSW, Social Worker

Carolyn Reyes, JD, MSW, Staff Attorney

Shannan Wilber, JD, Executive Director

National Center for Lesbian Rights

Courtney Joslin, JD, Senior Staff Attorney

Jody Marksamer, JD, Staff Attorney

Shannon Minter, JD, Legal Director

Model Standards Project Advisory Committee

Bill Bettencourt, *Stuart Foundation, **Annie E. Casey Foundation, San Francisco, CA

Craig Bowman, National Youth Advocacy Coalition, Washington, DC

Patricia Bresee, Retired San Mateo Juvenile Court Commissioner, Atherton, CA

Pam Connie, San Francisco Human Services Agency, San Francisco, CA

Mary Curtin, Private psychotherapy practice, Florence, MA

Terry DeCrescenzo, Gay and Lesbian Social Services, West Hollywood, CA

Ken Ellis, Missouri Division of Youth Services, Kansas City, MO

Rudy Estrada, Lambda Legal, New York, NY

Rebekah Evenson, Altshuler Berzon, San Francisco, CA

Charlie Fernandez, Tides Foundation, San Francisco, CA

Michael Ferrera, *GLASS, **LifeWorks Mentoring, West Hollywood, CA

Kate Frankfurt, Human Rights Watch, San Francisco, CA

Susan Hazeldean, Urban Justice Center, New York, NY

---

* Affiliation as of June 2003.   ** Current affiliation.

Jude Koski, California Youth Connection, San Francisco, CA

Lena Lopez, *Office of the Foster Care Ombudsperson, Sacramento, CA

Johnny Madrid, *California Youth Connection & Stanford University, Stanford, CA

Gerald P. Mallon, Hunter College School of Social Work, New York, NY

Martha Matthews, Children's Law Center, Los Angeles, CA

Carla Odiaga, *Lambert House, Seattle, WA, **Waltham House, Waltham, MA

Andrew Park, Wellspring Advisors, New York, NY

Anne Parsons, Juvenile Justice Project of Louisiana, New Orleans, LA

Nancy Polikoff, American University College of Law, Washington, DC

Maria Ramiu, Youth Law Center, San Francisco, CA

Gary Remafedi, Director, Youth and AIDS Projects, Professor, Department of Pediatrics, University of Minnesota, Minneapolis, MN

Caitlin Ryan, Cesar Chavez Institute, San Francisco State University, San Francisco, CA

Marlene Sanchez, Center for Young Women's Development, San Francisco, CA

Laurie Schaffner, Department of Criminal Justice, University of Illinois at Chicago, Chicago, IL

---

* Affiliation as of June 2003. ** Current affiliation.

Leslie Silver Hoffman, *Urban Justice Center, **HIV Law Project, New York, NY

Dean Spade, *Urban Justice Center, **Sylvia Rivera Law Project, New York, NY

Raquel Tolston, *California Youth Connection, San Francisco, CA

Raquel Volaco-Simoes, *Project OffStreets, Minneapolis, MN

Bill Womack, Children's Hospital and Regional Medical Center, Seattle, WA

Marynella Woods, Public Defender's Office, Juvenile Division, San Francisco, CA

Rob Woronoff, Child Welfare League of America, Washington, DC

---

* Affiliation as of June 2003. ** Current affiliation.